THE TRIUMPH OF LOVE

'Omnia vincit Amor: et nos cedamus Amori'
(Love conquers all; let us, too, yield to love!)
VIRGIL, *Eclogues*, X, 69

GEOFFREY C. MUNN

THE *TRIUMPH* OF *LOVE*

JEWELRY
1530-1930

with 115 illustrations
112 in color

THAMES AND HUDSON

ALEXANDRO · ET · EDVARDO · FILIIS · DILECTIS · PIGNVS · AMORIS · PATRII

Above, gold brooch in the form of a lovers' knot, which may have been inspired by the coloured love knots referred to in Virgil's *Eclogues* (VII, 75). The jewel is set with a dazzling collection of gemstones, including coloured diamonds, Mexican fire opals, pink topazes, tourmalines, aquamarines, emeralds, rubies, amethysts, and peridots. Probably English *c.* 1880.
(*Private collection, Memphis, Tennessee.*)

Half title, a ruby and diamond brooch in the form of a radiant heart.
English *c.* 1780. (*Mrs. A Kenneth Snowman.*)

Title page, Lovers embracing within a bower of gold branches and blue enamelled leaves. This ivory and gold brooch is typical of the elaborate yet delicate work of René Lalique, the master of Art Nouveau jewelry. The reverse of the jewel is similarly decorated with chased work.
Signed LALIQUE. (*Calouste Gulbenkian Museum, Lisbon.*)

© 1993 Thames and Hudson Ltd, London

First published in the United States of America in 1993 by
Thames and Hudson Inc., 500 Fifth Avenue,
New York, New York 10110

Library of Congress Catalog Card Number 93-60429

ISBN 0-500-23661-5

Printed and bound in Singapore

CONTENTS

PREFACE

From time immemorial, the incorruptibility of gold has symbolized the enduring qualities of true love. Similarly, the colour of precious stones has always been associated with the intensity of passion. It therefore follows that betrothal, marriage and anniversary are usually marked by a gift of jewelry; and the favourite choice on such occasions is the ring which, with no beginning and no end, neatly extends the metaphor.

The appreciation of colourful, small, rare and intensely valuable materials is akin to our fascination with flowers, and it is obvious that our spiritual qualities are reflected in the appreciation of many forms of natural beauty. This may explain why, despite the kaleidoscopic range of experience available to us today, the appeal of precious metals remains unabated; indeed, it is no coincidence that the recent illogical fashion for carrying crystals has gained momentum throughout the West at a time when more conventional creeds are losing their grip. Every aspect of art is now collected and studied with a degree of zeal which only just falls short of veneration; this may be an expression of the same spiritual repining which has encouraged a host of different religions.

In the groundswell of these trends, the collecting of jewelry and the study of its history have become more popular than ever before, and books devoted to the subject are available in abundance. Although some hesitation in adding to this plethora may be justifiable, little has been published in which the subject of love jewelry is investigated independently. Notable exceptions are *Sentimental Jewellery* by Shirley Bury (H.M.S.O, 1985), *The Art of the Jeweller* (British Museum Publications, 1984) and *Treasures and Trinkets, Jewellery in*

London from Pre-Roman Times to the 1930's (Museum of London, 1991). They refer exclusively to the collections of the Victoria and Albert Museum, the British Museum and the Museum of London respectively. I have drawn on these sources but have also illustrated and discussed jewelry from private collectors whenever possible.

I have not tried to make a specific examination of the emblematic significance ascribed to precious stones by lapidaries. Joan Evans's book *Magical Jewels of the Middle Ages and the Renaissance*, first published by the Clarendon Press in 1922, has recently been reprinted and scholars need look no further for a comprehensive account of this fascinating subject. However, when a particular precious stone contributes to the meaning of a jewel I have drawn the reader's attention to it.

If the strict definition of an anthology is a collection of flowers of verse, the pages which follow are indeed an anthology of love jewelry. This is not a truly comprehensive study of the subject, since the volume of material available is enormous. Rather, it is hoped that collectors and jewelers will find this small book useful not only in deciphering the more complicated allegories and rebuses of amatory jewelry, but also as a source of inspiration. For those with a more fundamental interest in the subject I hope that it will assume the role of the jewelry itself by becoming a treasured emissary of love in its own right.

INTRODUCTION

Full many a gem of purest ray serene
The dark unfathom'd caves of ocean bear;
Full many a flower is born to blush unseen,
And waste its sweetness on the desert air.
Thomas Gray (1716–71),
Elegy in a Country Churchyard

In much the same way as some animals will offer in courtship a morsel of food, there are some – the Bower bird, for instance – that will make gifts of feathers and flowers and all manner of rare and colourful trifles. There can be little doubt that the first tokens of human affection were of a similar nature and were worn as treasured souvenirs. Presumably skill and craftsmanship followed quickly and the intrinsic qualities of shells and stones were effectively enhanced. The evolution of jewelry had begun.

In antiquity it was Aphrodite who presided over love, beauty and generation, and a good part of the text which follows will be devoted to the revival of her cult. It is therefore necessary to give a brief résumé of love jewelry in the ancient world in order to place classical allusions in context.

It is likely that the knowledge of Aphrodite reached the Greek world from Cyprus in the Mycenaean age, but by the time of Homer (*c.* 700 BC) the Hellenization of the deity had begun. Her image was to appear increasingly, but perhaps never more dramatically in jewelry than on a gold medallion from South Russia which dates from the third century BC and is now in the Preussischer Kulturbesitz in Berlin. In this jewel she is accompanied by her familiar Eros, who is seen perched behind her left ear. It is often his winged presence which

proclaims the identity of the goddess, whereas he himself
rarely needs an introduction. In the British Museum alone,
there are over twenty gold 'Eros' figure earrings, ranging in
date from the fourth century BC to the first and second
centuries AD. In his catalogue of the ancient jewelry in the
Museum, F.H. Marshall[1] records that it is on this type of
ornament that the ancient jeweler lavished much of his
attention. Eros appears in several different guises, among
them Papposilenos and the horned Pan. In a pair of earrings
from Kyme in Aeolia, the smiling love-god carries a tablet on
which to record the names of lovers. Sometimes he is a
musician carrying a kithara, plectrum or syrinx. Elsewhere he
is an actor bearing a mask, and in another jewel he holds a
mirror case; in his most dangerous guise he turns a magic
wheel to subdue the heart with a potent spell of love.

In the ancient world, the mischievous winged boy
was also found in the company of Psyche. Rather than
inflicting torment on individuals, he sometimes turned his

attention to the goddess of the soul, since this was widely recognized as the seat of the passions. Psyche's symbol is the butterfly and this appears frequently in ancient jewelry – not only as a metaphor for higher emotion but also to exploit the decorative effect of the insect itself. Again, several examples can be found in the British Museum: two are particularly worthy of attention because they were well known in the nineteenth century and undoubtedly influenced the work of contemporary jewelers. The earliest dates from the third century BC and was excavated by Prince Torlonia at Vulci. It was later owned by the famous revivalist jeweler and antique dealer Alessandro Castellani, from whose posthumous sale it was purchased by the Museum in 1884. The other is a Roman necklace from the second century AD hung with a butterfly, the body and wings of which are set with cabochon garnets and sapphires; because of its immediate charm, it was the inspiration for more than one pastiche from the Castellani atelier.

Another motif frequently used by the classical jewelers was the knot of Hercules, since it was believed to have magical properties, presumably because it was a symbol of strength. However, there was a further significance which is relevant to our subject. The naked torsos of several of the boys decorating the 'Eros' earrings in the British Museum have breast bands tied with knots of Hercules, confirming an association with the allegory of love. The metaphor is simple: such knots are easily tied but are stronger than the material from which they are made. Many examples of this popular device have come down from antiquity, but among the necklaces and diadems, some set with cabochon garnets or decorated with granulation, there is one extraordinary survival: a breast band (now in the British Museum) that dates from the third century BC. Here the allegory is reversed and it is the band itself which is decorated with *amorini* carrying flaming torches, the whole centring on a *nodus Herculaneus* hung with gold pomegranates.[2]

Since rings were the usual tokens of betrothal and marriage, the knot of Hercules, with its general and specific symbolism, was an appropriate and attractive design with which to decorate the bezels. The Romans used the device to make the links of chains and these were sometimes interspersed with raw emerald crystal beads or pearls. Clasped hands were another symbol of commitment and spiritual unity, and these were widely used throughout the Roman Empire. They appear on the bezels of rings, either chased in gold or engraved on hardstones. Profile portraits of betrothed or married couples were also used in this way.

There is probably no justification for separating these amatory devices from the wider context of classical mythology and decoration. Neither should one isolate Aphrodite from her sister goddesses, the majority of whom involved themselves with love at some level. Indeed, Eros is only a step away from the pranks of Priapus and Dionysus. Here, however, such a narrow perspective is appropriate, because love jewelry, since the sixteenth century, has for reasons of propriety been mainly Aphrodisian in its inspiration.

For the purposes of this study, Aphrodite and Venus are treated as one and the same, as they were in classical Rome. By the same token, Cupid, the son of Mercury and Venus, is identified with Eros.

Evidence that jewelry and love were as closely associated in the ancient world as they are today can be found in a fascinating fresco from Pompeii. Just as Cupid is often seen at Vulcan's forge, so a group of *amorini* are engaged in a goldsmith's workshop making jeweled ornaments more subtly dangerous than arrows, with intent to wound a victim's heart.

Amorini in a goldsmith's workshop. The winged figure on the left of this Roman fresco painted in the first century BC is modelling a jewel with a hammer and anvil. Those on the right are melting gold in a crucible with the use of a blowpipe. The subject brings to mind Cupid making arrows at Vulcan's forge.
(*Casa dei Vettii, Pompeii. Photo Fotografico Foglia.*)

What thing is love for (well I wot) love is a thing.
It is a prick, it is a sting,
It is a pretty, pretty thing;
It is a fire, it is a coal
Whose flame creeps in at every hole.
George Peel (1558?–97?), *The Hunting of Cupid*

Until the first flowering of the Renaissance, patronage was largely in the hands of church and clergy. The delicate skills of the goldsmith were no exception and a large proportion of medieval jewelry is of a devotional nature. It has been suggested that, as far as goldsmiths' work is concerned, the Renaissance began in Italy in the second half of the fifteenth century.[3] The fashion for valuable ornaments was fostered by a new type of patron who was at once conspicuous, wealthy and passionate about the antique. Such attitudes were embodied in the Medici of Florence and the Sforza of Milan. Encouraged by the enthusiasm of these new patrons, the cult of Venus was revived. The young and handsome Giuliano de' Medici was the model for Botticelli's Mercury in the painting *Primavera* and Mars in *Mars and Venus*. Giuliano's tournament standard was Cupid tied to an olive tree with his bows and arrows broken at his feet – a witty allusion to the difficulties of the many who had tried to entice him into marriage.

Giuliano's elder brother, Lorenzo, though he was known as the Magnificent, was actually ill-proportioned and had a bad complexion and a hard, repellent voice. But for all these shortcomings he had heightened sensibilities, which found expression in the writing of poetry, much of it amorous, as is the following sonnet (translated by John Addington Symonds):

Leave thy beloved isle, thou Cyprian Queen;
 Leave thine enchanted realm so delicate,
 Goddess of Love! Come where the rivulet
Bathes the short turf and blades of tenderest green!

Come to these shades, these airs that stir the screen
 Of whispering branches and their murmurs set
 To Philomel's enamoured canzonet:
Choose this for thine own land, thy loved demesne!

And if thou com'st by these clear rills to reign,
 Bring thy dear son, thy darling son, with thee,
  For there be none that own his empire here.
From Dian steal the vestals of her train,
 Who roam the woods at will, from danger free,
  And know not love nor his dread anger fear.

Benvenuto Cellini, probably the best-known of the Renaissance goldsmiths, was born in 1500, eight years after Lorenzo's death. He was to exemplify the versatility of the Renaissance artist-craftsman, who was often trained not only as jeweler and goldsmith but also as painter and sculptor. Apprenticeship involved the mastery of many skills, including drawing, engraving, chasing, casting, enamelling and niello work. It was far from certain that a goldsmith's assistant would eventually become a goldsmith himself. Like Donatello and Ghiberti, some emerged as sculptors, or perhaps as painters, as Ghirlandaio and Andrea del Sarto did. Pollaiuolo and Verrocchio discovered that it was perfectly possible to work in several media, returning to goldsmithing and jewelry when required. It is for these reasons that Italian jewelry of the sixteenth century is particularly inspired and refined, and that it can be seen as a minute distillation of the fine arts.

The Garden of Love by Titian (*c.* 1490–1576), now in the Prado in Madrid, was painted sometime after 1518; *The Exposure of Luxury* by Angelo Bronzino (1503–72), which can be seen in the National Gallery in London, was finished in about 1545 and paid for by Cosimo de' Medici as a gift for François I of France. Bronzino's picture is an allegory of the futility and transience of love, and Titian's is a symbol of its careless pleasures. Bronzino was a friend of Cellini; they came from similar backgrounds and certainly shared some of the same patrons. It is not surprising that the goldsmiths of the sixteenth century were preoccupied with the same subject-matter as their fellow artists.

There is one aspect of the Renaissance which is particularly relevant to the art of the goldsmith and jeweler; that is the taste for emblems. The name emblem is usually given to a simple allegorical design accompanied by an explanatory motto, which was intended to teach an intuitive form of moral truth. Emblems originated in the hieroglyphs of ancient Egypt, and through the Alexandrian Greek world they found their way into the repertoire of European artists. These succinct and highly decorative devices were taken up with enthusiasm in the courts of Europe and used in many ways, including badges for servants, champions and livery-men. It is in this role, stitched in gold and silver to the back of uniforms, or decorating hats and caps, that they most closely echo Renaissance jewel work. Both devotional and amorous allusions are common, and even a cursory study of the subject reveals how the cult of Venus was followed in the fifteenth and sixteenth centuries. The charm of an emblem is that its significance was often comprehensible only to those already familiar with it. Nothing demanded covert expression more than the allegory of love, and Cupid is therefore portrayed in many guises. The banner of Giuliano de' Medici, previously referred to, is a typical example. In other emblems, the capricious god inflicts all manner of torments: lovers are racked, burned, pierced and hanged. Cupid himself is tied to trees, distills tears from his burning heart, consorts with wild

Titian's *The Garden of Love*, a celebration of careless pleasure.
(*Prado, Madrid.*)

beasts and is stung by bees. He reproduces himself by sowing seeds in the ground in a way which seems to anticipate the most alarming science fiction films. Such a wealth of inspiration is to be found in the art of the emblematist that jewelers and goldsmiths have continued to draw on it even to the present day. The two media are so closely related that some artists – Hans Holbein, for instance – dealt in both.

The Judgment of Paris. In this oval gold hat-badge of the mid-sixteenth century, Aphrodite is accompanied by Eros as she receives her prize of an apple and is crowned with laurels by a flying *amorino*. Hermes, standing behind the seated Paris, is identified by his winged helmet and caduceus wand. The disappointed losers in the competition, Hera (Juno) and Athene (Minerva), are on the right. The badge, Italian or possibly French, is decorated with enamel, later set with a peridot and a sapphire and a border of garnets and almandines. (*By permission of the Trustees of the British Museum.*)

In general, the emblematic artists chose the better-known mythology of the ancient world, and as a result their work was rich in amatory allusion. Paris, the son of Priam and Hecuba, is associated with a fable of choice, in which Hermes brought Hera, Athena and Aphrodite to him so that he might judge who was the most beautiful. In reality this was a contest between kingship, military prowess and love, and it goes without saying that love triumphed. The Judgment of Paris has been a recurring theme in art since the seventh century and enjoyed great popularity during the Renaissance. In the Waddesdon Bequest in the British Museum[5] there is a hat jewel devoted to this subject; probably Italian, dating from the mid-sixteenth century, it is a fine example of historiated Renaissance jewelry made in celebration of the cult of Aphrodite. A similar example is listed in 1566 among the jewels of the Medici court in Florence, and a lady, thought to be Princess Elizabeth, is shown wearing a related jewel in her portrait by Hans Holbein the Younger, dating from about 1543.

During the course of the Renaissance, the use of profane subject-matter in art became widespread. Goldsmiths and jewelers relied increasingly upon the design books prepared by artists which were available throughout Europe. It is possible that the decorative artists of the Renaissance had become more specialized and that the comprehensive training received in the Florentine workshops was no longer routine. Certainly the popularity of such design books has made the origins of sixteenth-century jewels difficult to determine. Nonetheless it is clear that some of the finest work comes from South Germany; in addition to religious subjects there are both direct and obscure allusions to love. Exactly like his fellow-artists in Florence, Albrecht Dürer (1471–1528) was trained as a goldsmith, and though no surviving jewel can be firmly attributed to his hand, a number of lively designs are to be found in the Louvre, the Kunsthallen of Bremen and Hamburg, and the Kupferstichkabinett in Berlin. Humanist themes are never seen in his jewel work, but his contemporary Lucas Cranach (1472–1553) painted a number of minutely detailed pictures of Venus for the Electors of Saxony in Württemberg. More often than not, the etiolated goddess is dressed in nothing but lavish gold belts and collars set with precious stones. The most evocative is the example in the National Gallery, London, entitled *Cupid Complaining to Venus*: here Cupid, having rashly pursued the cloying sweetness of the honeycomb and been punished by the bees who protect it, is seen seeking consolation from his mother. This is a charming allegory of pleasure and pain, and one which was also adopted by Hans Holbein in the design for a jewel now in the collection of the Duke of Devonshire (see p. 30). As we have already seen, this was also a favourite theme of the emblematists.

By the mid-sixteenth century, the pattern book artists, or *Kleinmeister*, as they were known, had infused the medium with fresh colour by the liberal suggestions of enamelling and precious stones in their designs. Those of Mathias Zundt are especially vivid, and were to be set with large cabochon and faceted gems supported by *amorini*, naturalistically enamelled in the round. Martin II Pfinzing was a designer of jewelry who

owed a debt to Dürer's inspiration; his Phoenix jewel is a particularly charming allegory of love revived.

Among the designers whose influence was greatest in South Germany during the second half of the century was Erasmus Hornick of Antwerp. In 1562 he published a design book entitled *The Love of the Gods*, providing inspiration for a number of his contemporaries in the jewelry trade. The entirely new type of frame evolved for German jewelry by 1565 has been ascribed to Hornick's influence. Gods and goddesses disport themselves in niches and are attended by *amorini* enclosed within the framework of the jewel.

An uncharacteristically light and romantic influence can sometimes be detected in German jewelry of the late sixteenth century and this may be due, at least in part, to a goldsmith and jeweler called Giovanni Battista Scolari working at the courts of Munich and Landshut.

Opposite, *Cupid Complaining to His Mother Venus*, by Lucas
Cranach. Cupid suffering from bee stings is a warning of the pain
which often accompanies the pleasure of love.
(*National Gallery, London.*)

The theme of Cupid stung by bees was used also by Hans Holbein
is this design for a hat-badge, which refers specifically in its
lettering to the pleasure and pain of love.
(*By kind permission of the Duke of Devonshire.*)

A splendid jewel in the shape of a gondola. The lovers within the canopy of the gold vessel, set with rubies, diamonds and pearls, are surrounded by the *commedia dell'arte* characters Pantalone and Zanne. The sides of the ship are decorated with forget-me-nots, which are emblematic of enduring passion. German, *c.* 1570. (*From the collection of the Elector Palatine in the Museo degli Argenti, Florence.*)

Scolari's visit to Germany coincided with the Duke and Duchess of Bavaria's invitation to Venetian actors to perform at the wedding of their son Wilhelm to Renata of Lorraine in 1568. Scolari was asked to take the part of one of the actors who had come to a violent end; he played Zanne in a Harlequinade opposite Orlando di Lasso as Messer Pantalone. Scolari is believed to have immortalized his only stage appearance by making the jewel now in the Museo degli Argenti in Florence, in which he is shown with Pantalone serenading the lovers.

According to Mario Praz in his fascinating *Studies in Seventeenth Century Imagery*, the sea-going vessel is a favourite allegory for an individual's triumph over the storms of love. The idea is paralleled in Shakespeare's Sonnet 116: '[Love] is the star to every wandering bark'. The self-consciously sentimental qualities of the Gondola jewels which have survived were successfully revived by Carlo Giuliano in

London in the second half of the nineteenth century (see p. 78). It may not be fanciful to suggest that he had seen a parallel between his own situation as a Latin in a northern land and that of Scolari during his stay in Munich.

The jeweler's art in the Low Countries had flourished on the wealth generated by trade in Antwerp. Still the diamond-cutting centre of the world today, in 1567 Antwerp boasted 124 working goldsmiths, innumerable lapidaries, and a highly successful trade in jewelry and precious stones. Dr Yvonne Hackenbroch, in her comprehensive survey *Renaissance Jewelry*, has identified a sixteenth-century workshop in Malines, then ruled by the Habsburg regent of the Netherlands, Margaret of Austria. From this workshop came a series of hat badges decorated with enamels, one of them a cynical but amusing comment on the relative attractions of love and money, a common subject in Flemish sixteenth-century painting. A comely wench in the fashionable clothes of the early 1500s is seen in the company of two men, one young, the other old. Round the jewel is a legend which translates as 'Love is something but money is everything.' This point of view is endorsed by the young lady, whose gaze is definitely in the direction of the older, presumably wealthier gentleman. His hand is placed, as if in affirmation, upon her heart. The hat badge is wrought from gold, the value of which subtly contributes to its meaning.

An enamelled gold hat-badge decorated with the scene of a young woman evidently choosing between two suitors, and bearing a cynical legend that implies that wealth matters more than love. From a workshop in Malines, Netherlands, *c.* 1520.
(*The Metropolitan Museum of Art, Robert Lehman Collection.*)

These two gold pendants feature an animal transfixed on an arrow. The one at left is a lion, its eyes and mouth set with cabochon and brilliant cut rubies respectively, which represents an allegory of love's power to subdue even the wild and strong. The body of the wounded beast is a large baroque pearl, and the enamelled pendant loop is hung with a single pearl. On the right, the victim is a stag, composed of three baroque pearls. This poignant jewel is believed to be an allegory of unrequited love. Flemish, *c.* 1575 and *c.* 1580. (*From the collection of the Elector Palatine in the Museo degli Argenti, Florence.*)

Rumbustious subject-matter of this nature is not necessarily a characteristic of Flemish Renaissance jewelry: a subtler, more touching note is more often struck. Typical examples in the Museo degli Argenti in Florence are allegories of the pain so often associated with affairs of the heart. One is a pendant in the form of a lion, the other a hind; both are agonizingly transfixed with arrows of gold. The lion is an allegory of strength and virtue but also of the bellicose spirit, generosity in victory and vigilance. Dr Hackenbroch and Maria Sprameli[6] have linked the wounded beast with an emblem that shows a tamed lion carrying an *amorino* on its

back, accompanied by Virgil's hemistich 'Omnia Vincit Amor' (Love conquers all). Love triumphing over strength is a recurrent theme in precious metalwork and glyptics; but in the lion jewel in Florence, the terrible wound inflicted on the beast makes his subjugation final. The suggestion is that love, however foreign to such a powerful wild beast, may subdue him all the more effectively when he finally succumbs.

The wounded hind jewel in the same collection carries an even more poignant message of the inescapability of unrequited love. Again the jewel has been associated with an emblem in which a running stag is pierced with an arrow. Accompanying it is the message, 'Hinc dolor, inde fuga, gravis' (Here pain, there flight, both unbearable).

The bodies of the animals in these jewels are represented by cleverly chosen baroque pearls, a favourite conceit of the Netherlandish goldsmiths in the second half of the sixteenth century.

The jewelers of the Low Countries also had a taste for good-natured and amusing representations of Cupid armed with a bow. The half-dozen or so which have survived are all naturalistically enamelled in the round and profusely set with precious stones; some of these jewels incorporate the doves of Venus and occasionally clasped hands. The example now in the collection of Baron Thyssen-Bornemisza is especially capricious; Cupid's aim is rendered completely random by a blindfold of blood-red rubies. There is some evidence that these enchanting jewels were made for export. A portrait of Isabella, daughter of Philip II of Spain, shows her wearing one pinned to her bodice; complete with pendant pearl, it is closely paralleled by the examples in the Rijksmuseum in Amsterdam and the Hermitage State Museum in St Petersburg.

The role of the Renaissance artist-craftsman was filled in England by Hans Holbein the Younger (1497/8–1543). He was court artist to Henry VIII, and created what has become posterity's image of the King. His paintings are characterized by an impassive realism and his designs for goldsmiths' work by a seemingly careless facility. He achieved symmetry and pattern despite the constraints his patrons inevitably imposed. Initial letters and monograms are made into satisfying

In this portrait of Isabella, daughter of Philip II of Spain, she is wearing a pendant in the form of Cupid armed with bow and arrow (see detail below). The jewel is strikingly similar to a gold enamelled pendant of *c.* 1590 (right), set with rubies, diamonds and pearls, and suspended from a cartouche in the form of the doves of Venus contesting a red enamel heart. (*Portrait by Gracious Permission of H.M. the Queen; pendant Netherlandish, Rijksmuseum, Amsterdam.*)

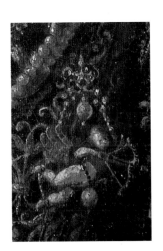

pendant shapes, and precious stones are stylishly wrapped in mottoes and true lovers' knots. The emblem, possibly the design for a hat badge, at Chatsworth in the form of a blindfolded Cupid who has been stung by bees, shows that Holbein was as fascinated with the allegory of love as were his contemporaries.

When Queen Mary I came to the throne after the fleeting reign of Edward VI (1547–53), she brought with her a revival of the Catholic religion, and her preference was almost exclusively for jewelry of liturgical significance. Mary did, however, own a brooch given to her by her father on 24 July 1546, which depicts the story of Pyramus and Thisbe and was set with a large table-cut diamond. The choice of subject is ironic, since it illustrates the ultimate sacrifice to passionate love – something in which the Queen was deluded by her ambitious husband, Philip II of Spain. Pyramus and Thisbe, according to the Latin poet Ovid, lived next door to one another and, failing their parents' permission to marry, whispered to each other through the cracked wall between the two houses. Eventually they agreed to meet at the tomb of Nimus and there Thisbe was frightened by a blood-stained lion. She dropped her cloak as she ran and the wild beast mauled it. Pyramus, finding the gory remains of the garment, believed she was dead and killed himself in grief. Later, Thisbe returned and, finding her lover's body, followed his desperate example. Their blood stained the leaves of the mulberry tree, whose sanguine fruit has ever since turned black when ripe, in mourning for the tragic lovers.

Mary I died in 1558 and the religious pendulum swung once again in favour of the Protestant Church and with it a new enthusiasm for the monarchy. Elizabeth knew the value of ostentatious wealth to her image; only weeks after her sister's death she passed through the streets of London in unparalleled splendour on the way to her coronation. As she grew older, the Queen became an icon tricked out each morning with powder, wigs, silks, gold, pearls and diamonds. Sir Francis Bacon recorded, 'She imagined that the people, who are much influenced by externals, would be diverted by the glitter of her jewels from noticing the decay of her

personal attractions' – a point of view echoed three centuries later by Sir Roy Strong: 'No other English monarch had such an obsession with her own stage management.'[7]

A glance at any of the dozens of surviving portraits will reveal how richly she is dressed in far-fetched silks, furs and jewels. The majority of her ornaments served some emblematic function but were rarely of an amatory nature. Elizabeth clearly felt herself increasingly wedded to her country, and as the possibility of a real marriage receded, her jewelry sometimes made covert reference to virginity, the most obvious symbols of which were the sieve and the ermine. From time to time, however, the Queen was given jewelry in remembrance of love and friendship. After the death of her favourite, the Earl of Leicester, in 1588, she received a farewell gift of 'A magnificent jewel, ablaze with emeralds and diamonds and attached to a rope of six hundred white pearls, worth in all a thousand marks'.[8] This remarkable object is now lost but we can be certain that Elizabeth was deeply moved when she received it.

It was also the Queen's habit to make gifts of jewelry. More often than not, they bore her image as either an engraved gem, a miniature, or a medal. There is some evidence to suggest that it was she who gave the pendant which is now known as the Gresley Jewel to Catherine Walsingham when she married Sir Thomas Gresley. It is a miniature case of architectural form set centrally with a cameo of a female blackamoor, possibly seen as an exotic Venus. She is flanked by black *amorini*, each emerging from a cornucopia and loosing the arrows of love from longbows. These elements anticipate the fruitful union of Sir Thomas and Lady Gresley, whose miniature portraits by Nicholas Hilliard are contained within the pendant.

By far the most dramatic and enigmatic jewel to survive from the sixteenth century is the Darnley, or Lennox, Jewel, which now belongs to Queen Elizabeth II. It was thought to have been made for the Countess of Lennox, Lady Margaret Douglas, in order to send coded messages of love to her husband Matthew Stuart, Earl of Lennox, when he was Regent of Scotland. Dr Hackenbroch believes that it is more

Tradition has it that Queen Elizabeth I gave this oval gold pendant to Catherine Walsingham, niece of her secretary of state Sir Francis Walsingham, upon the occasion of her wedding to Sir Thomas Gresley. Devoted to the theme of love and containing miniatures of the couple by Elizabeth's court limner Nicholas Hilliard, the pendant is set with rubies, emeralds and pearls; the front is set with a striated agate cameo of a black woman (possibly seen as a portrait of Venus). This theme is taken up by the two black *amorini*, armed with bows and arrows, which emerge from a cornucopia on each side of the jewel. English, *c.* 1585. (*Pennington Mellor Munthe Charitable Trust.*)

likely to be a memorial jewel for her husband, who was killed in 1571, or perhaps as a gift for her royal grandson who was later to become James I of Scotland. The heart-shaped sapphire with which it is set determines the outline of the jewel, and its gold surface is entirely covered with emblems of sacred and profane love, heightened with several different types of enamelling.

The Lennox or Darnley jewel, a gold pendant with a wealth of emblems and devices of sacred and profane love, appears to refer to the life of Margaret Douglas, Countess of Lennox, and the pretensions of young James VI of Scotland to the throne of England. In the centre is a crowned and winged heart surrounded by four allegorical figures: bottom left, Faith with the Cross and Lamb; top left, Victory with the Olive Branch; top right, Truth with a mirror; and below, Faith with the Cross. The crown over the heart opens to reveal two hearts united by a blue buckle and a golden true lovers' knot pierced with arrows, feathered with white enamel and tipped with gold. The reverse of the jewel is decorated with several emblematic devices, including the sun in splendour, a crowned salamander, and the phoenix in flames. The jewel, made about 1575, is decorated with enamel and set with a cabochon sapphire, table-cut rubies and an emerald. *(Reproduced by Gracious Permission of H.M. the Queen.)*

By the end of Elizabeth's reign, the colonization of which she was so proud had a profound influence on the art of the goldsmith and jeweler. Both England and her enemy Spain had scoured the world for treasure and returned with gold and emeralds from the New World. Furthermore, Oriental stone merchants were attracted to the West, bringing Burmese rubies, Indian emeralds, water white diamonds from the Golconda mines in Hyderabad and pearls from the Persian Gulf. These were polished, faceted and drilled, and became the focal point of jewelry which, until then, had been of a more sculptural and symbolic nature. In short, Mannerism had given way to the splendour of the Baroque.

Love is a circle that doth restless move
In the same sweet eternity of love.
    Robert Herrick (1591–1674),
    Love What It Is

After the far-reaching advances and political upheavals of the sixteenth century, Europe was a different and less integrated entity. Some of the northern countries, as a result of deepening religious convictions, had broken utterly with the Catholic south. New scientific concepts, under the influence of Copernicus, Galileo, Vesalius and Bacon, helped to erode medieval notions. John Donne said, 'The new philosophy calls all in doubt.'

It was an age of renewed classicism, to be exploited by great painters from Holland, Flanders, France and Spain. Rembrandt, Rubens, Van Dyck, Claude, Poussin and Velasquez were as well known as any of their Italian contemporaries. Aphrodisian themes continued to preoccupy artists and craftsmen, but the attention of the jeweler was largely devoted to newly discovered materials. In painting, too, the wonders of the natural world appeared to dwarf humanity itself. Rather as the lovers in Claude's *Acis and Galatea* are overwhelmed by a glorious sunset, so the emblems of love were often eclipsed by the colour and scintillation of precious stones. This is graphically illustrated in a design for a *sévigné* or bodice ornament by Gilles Légaré, which is dated 1663. It takes the form of a large drooping bow with a long trail of ribbons to be entirely set with rose-cut diamonds. From it hang two small

Sainct Denis en France

The bow in the design at left for a *sévigné* or bodice ornament may be interpreted as a true lovers' knot, and the seal-shaped pendants which hang from it are decorated with the roses of Venus and a heart tied with snakes, emblematic of eternal love. The great number of diamonds with which the jewel is to be set have almost obscured its amorous message. By Gilles Légaré, dated 1663. (*The Victoria and Albert Museum.*)

seals, one in the form of roses sacred to Venus, the other a heart tied with snakes symbolizing eternity. They are a reference to the bow itself, which is undoubtedly seen as an extension of the true-lovers' knot. However, the message is almost lost in the boldness of the design and the richness of the diamond work.

However, there is an exception to this general rule: it is a seventeenth-century gem-set jewel, now in the Victoria and Albert Museum, London, which successfully combines the use of precious stones with an unambiguous message of love. Made in a Prague workshop in the Hungarian manner in the early part of the seventeenth century, it is cleverly arranged as an archery target of diamonds, rubies and emeralds, the centre of which is a crowned heart carved from a single large ruby pierced by two of Cupid's arrows. The reverse of the jewel contains a miniature of a man who is presumably the victim of the passions to which the jewel alludes.

Above, three jeweled bows from the Cheapside Hoard which can be interpreted as conventionalized lovers' knots. The brooch in the centre is of silver set with 'opal' and 'diamond' pastes. The gold brooch on top is set with diamonds and two rubies, and the one below is of gilt metal set with garnets. English, *c.* 1600. (*The Museum of London.*)

The symbolism and magical significance of precious stones were still highly considered in the seventeenth century. For example, pearls are the typical adornment of the Goddess of Love, and the earrings, one black and one white, worn by Rubens's *Venus before a Mirror*, now in the collection of the Prince of Liechtenstein, stand for the dark and light side of passion. This is a message endorsed by the voluptuous painting of Maria Mancini by Jacob Ferdinand Voet (*c*.1639–1700?), now in the Staatliche Museen in Berlin. The subject is wearing a single row of large pearls as a necklace, together with pearl girandole earrings; she holds in her right hand another pearl suspended from a red silk cord, presumably in moody contemplation of the giver. Despite the wealth of material from the New World, the magical and metaphorical significance of precious stones in seventeenth-century jewelry was sometimes expressed in the most modest and intimate of ways. Chief among these was the finger ring; the most evocative of the various types were called 'gimmel fede'. *Gimmel* comes from 'gemellus', a twin, and *fede* from the old Italian 'mani in fede' (which means 'hands in faith'). In the collection of Baron Thyssen-Bornemisza there is a fine example in the form of an enamelled heart held between the fingers of two hands. Emblematic of betrothal, its form is based on Roman prototypes, but it is more sophisticated in being hinged, opening to reveal mottoes of faithfulness and emblems of mortality. The ruby and diamond with which the heart is set stand for the virtues in marriage of reconciliation and good humour.

Of all the seventeenth-century love rings, the most readily identified are those with amatory inscriptions, called posy (*poesy* or *poetry*) rings. These had their origins in the Middle Ages and were then called 'resons'; but from about 1430 they became known as posies, because of the cryptic messages with which they are engraved. Generally naive and charming, their idiosyncratic phraseology and spelling have a special appeal for collectors. Those from the seventeenth and eighteenth centuries are invariably quite plain on the exterior, in the manner of a traditional wedding ring; the legend, known only to the lovers, is engraved within. Some of the typical posies were: 'A Kiss for This', 'A Loving Wife Prolongeth Life', 'Live as I or else I Die', 'All Thine Is Mine', 'In Love at Night Is My Delight', 'In Thee a Flame; in Me the Same'.

The late Joan Evans was an enthusiastic collector of posy rings and made a special study of their inscriptions in *English Posies and Posy Rings* (London 1932). By the early nineteenth century the fashion was over, but the jewelers of today might easily revive the charming custom with a minimum of effort.

In contrast to the relatively simple charm of posies, there are some amusing and highly decorative rings which have come down to us from the seventeenth century. Among those in the Victoria and Albert Museum is an openwork band of gold, made to contain a lock of hair, which is decorated with brightly enamelled love birds; it dates from about 1675. Another is in the form of a gold band chased with a hare pursued by hounds, which is inscribed 'Time Lesseneth Not My Love'. It was made in England in mid-century.

A similarly light-hearted mood is characteristic of the unique cache of jewelry which has come to be called the Cheapside Hoard and is the most important source of our knowledge of Jacobean jewelry. Concealed in the 1640s and rediscovered in 1912, it is the elaborate stock-in-trade of a jeweler and comprises engraved gems, watches, fan holders, long chains, earrings and rings. The jewels are mainly enamelled and the stones with which they are set include turquoises, amethysts, rock crystals, garnets and the finest emeralds. This collection includes a number of jewels which

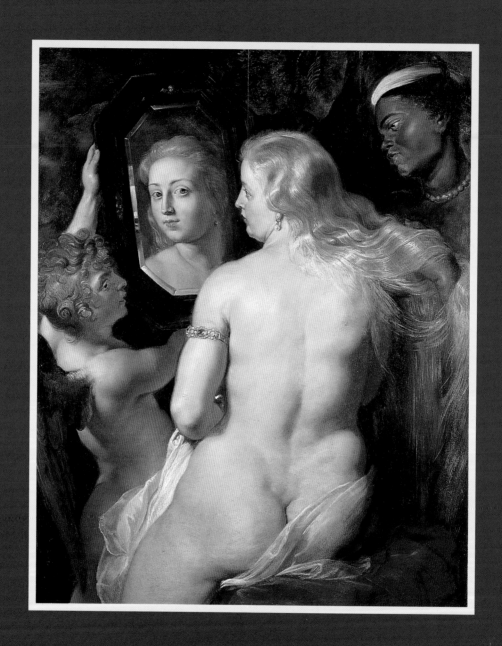

Opposite, in *Venus before a Mirror* by Peter Paul Rubens (1577–1640), the goddess of love is wearing a black and a white pearl earring, emblematic of the dark and light sides of passion. The white pearl is visible in actuality (see detail above), but the black pearl Venus is admiring can only be seen reflected in the mirror. About her upper arm, she wears a gold bracelet decorated with arrows and embellished with pearls and a large ruby, emblematic of passionate love. Oil on wood, c. 1616. (*The Collection of His Serene Highness the Prince of Liechtenstein, Vaduz Castle.*)

A portrait of Maria Mancini, niece of the powerful Cardinal Mazarin and beloved of King Louis XIV. Her beauty is accentuated here by her fine collection of pearl jewelry, though the necklace and girondole earrings do not appear to be as precious to her as the single pearl, presumably a treasured gift, which she holds in her right hand (see detail below). The white pearl has many meanings, among them innocence, purity and perfection. It is also one of the attributes of Venus and alludes to her birth from the sea. Painted by Jacob Ferdinand Voet. (*Staatliche Museen, Berlin.*)

are emblematic of both the sacred and the profane. Emblems of the Passion were offered alongside enamelled and gem-set salamanders symbolizing passionate love. Long gold daisy chains, symbolic of purity, are decorated with white enamel and set with garnets, and true lovers' knots are tied in opals, diamonds and red spinels.

The Cheapside Hoard has survived in fact, but the jewels of Queen Anne of Denmark, wife of James I of England and VI of Scotland, survive only in our imaginations. The inventory of her collection, compiled in 1606, is preserved in the National Gallery of Scotland. It provides a tantalizingly detailed account of an early seventeenth-century princely collection of jewelry now completely dismantled or dispersed. Among the jewels were dozens of pieces inspired by love. Their symbolism seems to have derived from the art of the emblematist, and there were seventeen jewels in the form of knots, nine in the form of hearts, two pierced with arrows, together with a number whose meaning is more obscure. These include pansies, snakes, a phoenix and a crossbow decorated with a heart. Five jewels in the form of a ship are recorded and were probably similar to those by Scolari, described earlier. But of all Queen Anne's love jewels, by far the most evocative is that described as follows: 'A Jewell of gold being a half circle with a candlestick and candle burning, two flies about the light, hanging at two small chains, the knoppes and Jewell garnished with small Diamonds of divers cuttes, with two small Pearles pendants, and iiij fixed; its weight 13 dwt. 11 grs.' This jewel was broken up by command of the Queen on 27 September 1610 so that the gold could be used to make a bowl.[9] Diana Scarisbrick has associated this jewel with a motto, dated 1635, which warns against the dangers of desire:

'*When you doe next behold the wanton Flyes*
About the shining candle, come to play,
Until the light thereof hath dimm'd their Eyes,
Or, till the flame hath sing'd their Wings away:
Remember, then, this Emblem; and beware
Your be not playing at such harmefull Games.'

Hair, an authentic and almost imperishable souvenir of the giver, has been associated with love and commemoration since antiquity. In the sixteenth century, woven strands of hair were tied about the wrist and secured by a ring on the finger, as well as being used for all sorts of ornamental trifles to decorate a lady's costume or coiffure. However, it was from the early 1600s that the subject began to assume greater significance, and this is echoed in the words of the seventeenth-century poet Théophile de Viau in *L'Ode à un Sien Amy*:

> '*Là, d'une passion ny jeune, ny legère*
> *J'aurais donné ma flamme aux yeux d'une bergère*
> *Dont le coeur innocent eust contente voeux*
> *D'un bracelet de chanvre avec ses cheveux.*'

In the Museum of London there is a rare survival in the form of an ear pendant, which dates from the early seventeenth century. It takes the form of a red enamelled heart from which hangs a single lock of hair, said to be that of King Charles I. Charlotte Gere has compared it to a similar jewel in the portrait of Anne, Lady Morton, datable to about 1620, which shows how it was probably worn.[10] In the *Portrait of Sir Thomas Aston at the Deathbed of His Wife* by John Souch, two versions are seen, both in black-and-white enamel, one decorated with a skull. Clearly memorial jewels, they illustrate how closely the commemoration of love and of death were

Moths fluttering round a candle flame; two have already been singed and lie at the foot of the candlestick. This circular gold brooch, set with a diamond and decorated with enamelling, is an allegory of the danger of passionate love. It is probably based on an unrecorded seventeenth-century prototype; a version was owned by Queen Anne of Denmark.
English *c.* 1880.
(*Clayre Armytage, London.*)

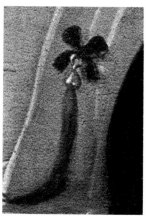

Locks of hair are often found in commemorative love jewelry. In this painting by John Souch, *Sir Thomas Aston at the Deathbed of His Wife*, Lady Aston, seen at the bottom right as she appeared in life, is wearing a lock of hair suspended from a small silver heart and a black silk bow (see detail right below). The jewel bears a striking resemblance to the heart-shaped pendant (right above), decorated in translucent enamel, with a lock of brown hair which is traditionally believed to be that of King Charles I (1600–49). It was handed down with a circumstantial account of its history: 'Ruby [enamel?] earring, *c.* 1640, heart-shaped with a lock of

Charles I's hair . . . given by Queen Henrietta Maria to her page Ralph Creyke and preserved ever since in the Creyke family.' (Painting *City of Manchester Art Galleries*; jewel given to *The Museum of London* by Mrs Walter Creyke in 1947.)

The heart-shaped gold locket decorated with red enamel was made by Carlo and Arthur Giuliano in the late nineteenth century; it appears to have been based on seventeenth-century models such as the one shown below it. (*Wartski, London.*)

associated in the seventeenth century. A touching example of this took place when Count Palatine Otto Heinrick died in 1604. His wife placed a pair of bracelets in his grave, one bearing her initials and the other a pair of hands cherishing a heart, all picked out in white enamel. Almost certainly these had been a gift of love from husband to wife, and the Countess Dorothea made a final gesture of devotion by returning them.[11]

Hair was also contained in lockets in conjunction with painted miniatures, and such a pendant jewel is seen in the *Portrait of an Unknown Gentleman* by Isaac Oliver (*c.* 1560–1617). The subject holds it in his hand, in what we must assume is an attitude of amorous contemplation, since he is seen against a background of flames which are emblematic of passion.

However, the most common use of hair in jewelry in the second half of the century was as a woven background to gold ribbon slides. These were generally made as mourning jewels; the initials of the departed are laid out in pearls or coloured foil over plaited hair, and the whole is glazed by a piece of faceted rock crystal. As we have already seen, some of the designs and techniques used in mourning jewelry were borrowed for a happier kind of sentimentality. In the Museum of London there is just such a slide containing hair, which shows Venus with a broken bow and Cupid running away with a heart. Below this charming scene is the legend 'Stop Theif'.

A pendant in the form of a salamander, which was thought to thrive in fire and is therefore an emblem of passionate love. This Spanish jewel dating from about 1600 is decorated with enamel and set with diamonds. (*S.J. Phillips, London.*)

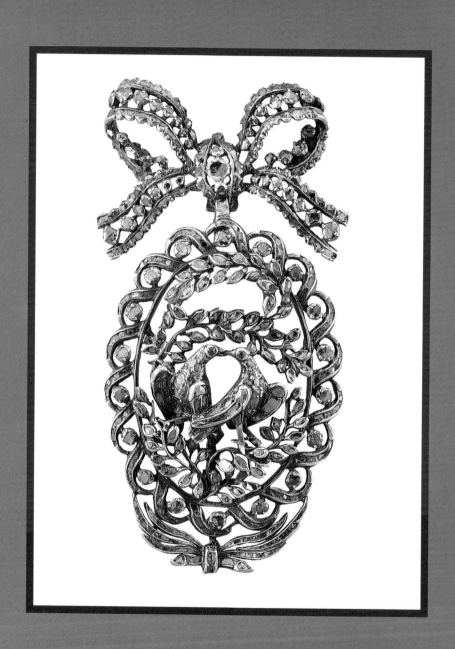

Opposite, the doves of Venus
and the laurels surrounding them
in this elaborate silver brooch
are emblematic of the Triumph
of Love, while the bow and the
palms stand for strength and
peace. The jewel is entirely set
with diamonds except for the
doves' eyes, which are
naturalistically represented by
rubies. French, *c.* 1760.
(*Private collection.*)

THE
EIGHTEENTH
CENTURY

Two doves hold each
end of a true lovers'
knot in the oval bezel
of this gold ring, which
is set with an ivory
plaque decorated with
pulverized hair. The
scene bears a legend,
'The farther I fly the
faster we tye'.
English, *c.* 1780.
(*Donohoe, London.*)

I had a dove and the sweet dove died;
And I have thought it died of grieving:
What could it grieve for? Its feet were tied,
With a silver thread of my own hands' weaving.
John Keats (1795–1821), *Song*

The eighteenth century has been described as the age of light
and lightness both in the decorative arts and in the mind.[12]
Candlelight encouraged the creation of lavish interiors, which
were often decorated with Chinese wallpapers, Oriental
porcelain, painted ceilings and damask hangings. Society
dress was equally luxurious; both ladies and gentlemen wore
satin and silk, some of the finest of which was made by the
Huguenots of Spitalfields. Cuffs were of lace and attention was
drawn to shoes by buckles of gold and diamonds.

The fashion for décolleté dresses allowed for an
extravagant display of necklaces or stomachers set with
coloured stones and diamonds. The variety of precious
materials available to the jeweler was even greater than in the
seventeenth century, since Russian aquamarines and
amethysts were available and Siberian emeralds were of a
finer colour than those from South America. As three-
dimensional forms were lost in the brilliance of the stones,
designs became bolder in order to be more readily understood. True lovers' knots were conventionalized into bows
which, in their noblest form, were diamond-set and worn in
threes, graduated to follow the line of the bodice. Earrings

inherited their shape from the Baroque and sometimes
incorporated emblems of the arts and sciences as well as those
of love.

Owners frequently remodelled their jewels to accommo-
date newly acquired gemstones in the latest fashion. As a
result, eighteenth-century diamond jewelry is rare, and that
which is emblematic of love rarer still. One example owes its
survival to the slaty quality of the stones and the fact that a
number of them were cut specifically to fit the composition.
Designed as a rebus for 'The Triumph of Love', it illustrates
the renewed enthusiasm for Aphrodisian themes encouraged
by Madame de Pompadour and her favourite artist, François
Boucher (1703–70). Under their influence, every available
surface seemed to be decorated with flaming hearts, hymenal
lamps, quivers and bows. In a series of wall panels by
Boucher's contemporary Jean Honoré Fragonard, now
preserved in the Frick Collection, New York, Cupid has
apparently learned a new trick to play on the doves of Venus:
he lunges at them viciously with a knife.

As a rule, the casting, chasing and enamelwork which
had been characteristic of sixteenth- and seventeenth-century
pieces were employed only on more modest jewelry – that
which the French call *bijouterie*. The masters of these delicate
crafts were obliged to resort to a variety of costume
accessories, including buttons, châtelaines, nécessaires,
watches, patch cases, bonbonnières and, above all, gold snuff

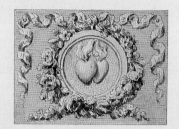

These watercolour designs are for a snuff box decorated with allusions to the Triumph of Love. On the sides are the traditional garlands of roses and laurels, as well as the doves of Venus. On the lid is a device of twinned flaming hearts garlanded with roses, sacred to Venus, and surmounted by a trailing lovers' knot. Paris, *c.* 1760. (*The Victoria and Albert Museum. Photograph courtesy of A. Kenneth Snowman Esq.*)

boxes. These small, valuable and highly decorated objects seem to parallel the sometimes secret nature of love and provided enduring evidence of it when offered as a gift. Not surprisingly a good number of them illustrate the cult of Venus with painted miniatures, enamels, chasing and even precious stones. The Album of Jean Ducrollay and His Followers,[13] recently acquired by the Victoria and Albert Museum, includes a design for a Louis XV snuff box to be rendered in pink enamel with twinned flaming hearts, rose garlands and doves, all of which are emblematic of passionate love. During the reign of Louis XVI, these allusions became slightly less obvious and *amorini* are more often seen involving themselves in the arts and sciences or in quiet contemplation of a landscape. Of all the designs used by eighteenth-century goldsmiths in the making of snuff boxes, perhaps the most charming and relevant to this discussion are those in the form of a letter, apparently folded, addressed and sealed. The hinged covers open to reveal a miniature or messages of passionate love. They may well have had their origins in the workshops of Alexander Fromery of Berlin, whose opaque white enamel boxes in the shape of all kinds of novelties are easily recognizable by their raised ornament applied with silver and gold. By the late eighteenth century, the style had been assimilated by the Russians and the French, and the example illustrated here was probably intended as a souvenir of Venice.

An enamelled copper snuff box with gilt metal mounts in the form of a love letter. It opens to reveal the following text: 'Tu às etès Le premier objet/qui pofsedet mon Coeur,/et regnoit sur mon Ame:/et Sera le dernier sujet/de mes Soupiers et de ma Flâme.' Loosely translated, it reads as follows: 'You are the first owner of my heart and you reign over my soul. You will be the last subject of my sighs and my desire.' The style of the French text suggests that it was composed by an Italian. French, *c.* 1780. (*Private collection.*)

In England in the 1760s there was a fashion for all sorts of agate snuff boxes and étuis which were mounted in gold in the rococo manner and with amatory legends in gold lettering against a white enamel ground. Invariably in French and often referring to love in separation, some typical inscriptions are: 'L'Amour expire l'amitié jamais', 'Gage de l'amitié', 'Si j'avois des Yeux', 'L'Amitié en fait le Prix', 'Fidèle en Amitié', 'Loin de vous rien agréable'.

An allegory of the folly and faithfulness of love: the figure of the Fool is seen teasing a pug dog, emblematic of faithfulness, by the tail; his gold buttons and buckles are ornamented with rose diamonds and his white collar bears the legend: 'Ils sont indissolubles' (They are inseparable). The collar on the dog bears a similar legend: 'L'Amitié me guide' (Love guides me). This unusually animated gold-mounted double agate scent bottle is English, dating from the mid-1760s. It clearly derives from Meissen porcelain types inspired by the *Commedia dell'arte* modelled by Johann Joachim Kaendler *c*. 1735–40, and in this instance the figure of Harlequin has been transformed into the Fool.
(*Private collection.*)

By far the most remarkable examples of this genre are a group of miniature sculptures in agate which are emblematic of the virtues of love. Of these the most important to have come to light is a double scent bottle; it derives from a Meissen group of Harlequin and his dog, but the meaning of the composition has been subtly altered by the anonymous eighteenth-century goldsmith who made it. In this case the scent bottle stands for the 'Folly and Faithfulness of Love', and the allegory is endorsed by the legends on the collars of the figures. There is some evidence to suggest that the lapidary work of this lively composition is German and that only the mounts are English. Although the dog has stood for faithfulness since classical antiquity, the German goldsmiths seem to have been especially fond of the metaphor. Snuff boxes in the form of recumbent pug dogs are common and are found in silver, gold, and carved from semi-precious stones. An example in the Hermitage Museum in St Petersburg is in green jasper and carries the legend SIEMPRE FIDEL (sic) on its collar.[14]

A white dog and other various emblems of passionate and faithful love are found in profusion in a neo-classical watch and fob commissioned by the Empress Joséphine from the famous Dresden goldsmith Johann Christian Neuber (1736–1808) as a gift to Napoleon. Its surface is entirely covered with a type of decoration called *Zellenmosaik*, which is made up of semi-precious stones laid flush with the surface of the gold. This technique is far enough removed from conventional mosaics to give the effect of champlevé enamel. It is peculiar to the workshops of Neuber, his father-in-law Heinrich Taddel, who is credited with its invention, and one Christian-Gottlieb Stiehl. The watch and fob has been dated to 1804–05 by Walter Holzhausen, and since the Imperial couple were married in 1796 it is tempting to suggest that the Empress had a wedding anniversary gift in mind. The quality of workmanship and the jewel-like intensity of this object seem to belie its date of manufacture, and the body of work to which it belongs is most definitely eighteenth-century.

By the 1760s neo-classicism had supplanted the rococo, and the Neuber watch and fob is the apogee of the new style.

The Empress Joséphine commissioned this gold watch and fob, a celebration of love, as a gift for Napoleon Bonaparte. The work of Johann Christian Neuber, it is entirely set with coloured hardstones, including carnelian, jasper, turquoise, lapis lazuli, quartzite, agate and iron pyrites in a technique known as *Zellenmosaik*. The watch case is decorated with the doves of Venus perched on a garlanded quiver of arrows, and the central reserve is bordered with triumphal laurels and forget-me-nots. The fob is composed of quatrefoil links from which the following can be read: Tendre, Sincere, Fidel, Secret, Ardent, Constant. They are gathered by a shaped gold plaque, decorated with flaming hearts tied together, surrounded by a garland of triumphal laurels. From this hang three additional lengths of chain with the legend, 'Uni pour toujours'. The circular plaques which join the chain at intervals bear symbols of the virtues already outlined. Thus the heart is tender, the mirror truthful, the dog faithful, the padlock secret, the flaming altar passionate, the tower constant.

On the reverse, the fob is decorated with forget-me-nots and laurels together with Cupid's arrows and the lamp of love. Attached to the fob are a pair of seals, one decorated with the first lovers Adam and Eve, the other with an owl in a cage, emblematic of love's dominion over wisdom. The watch key is in the form of a butterfly, a symbol of the soul. Here it is an allusion to time flying but love remaining.

The watch opens when a hidden trigger is pressed and reveals a portrait of Joséphine by Jean-Baptiste Isabey. Dresden, 1804–05. (*Private collection, photograph Wartski, London.*)

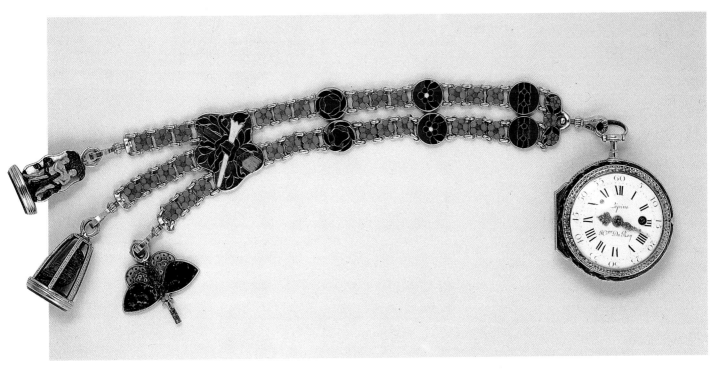

A pair of bracelet clasps, one decorated with the doves of Venus above Cupid's quiver, Hymen's lamp and a forget-me-not, the other with the monogram MA for Marie-Antoinette. The jewels are mounted in gold and set with brilliant cut diamonds. Marie-Antoinette was eighteen when she married the future Louis XVI, and she may have given these clasps to one of her ladies to mark the wedding. (*The Victoria and Albert Museum.*)

Shuttle-shaped jewels decorated with blue enamel or glass overlaid with diamonds are more frequently found. The bracelet clasps reproduced here were probably made in celebration of the marriage of Marie Antoinette to the Dauphin who was to become Louis XVI of France. One of them is decorated with Cupid's quiver, the lamp of love, forget-me-nots, and the doves of Venus; the other bears the Princess's cipher. Both are surmounted by the wreath of Trianon symbolizing the splendours of the French crown. Shirley Bury has suggested that they were given by Marie Antoinette to one of her ladies to mark the marriage which, she succinctly points out, was launched in brilliance and ended with the guillotine. Such neo-classical forms were popular in England too and were used on jewelry at all levels of importance. The largest group to have survived are mourning

In a sepia painting framed by an oval gold locket, Cupid is seen hovering about the altar of Venus, on which twinned flaming hearts have been transfixed by an arrow from his bow. The doves of Venus look on from a place of safety. English, *c.* 1780 (*Wartski, London.*)

jewels, which were often decorated with plaited or pulverized hair in the form of weeping willows, urns and the traditional paraphernalia of death. Among them, just as in the seventeenth century, there are a few which, though made in exactly the same way, seem to have more to do with love than commemoration.

In the eighteenth century the ring was still the most significant of all love tokens, its unbroken circle continuing to stand for mutual commitment and eternal regard. From the 1790s, the message was sometimes reinforced by a clever arrangement of coloured stones, the initial letters of which spell a term of endearment. Typically they are as follows: Ruby, Emerald, Garnet, Amethyst, Ruby and Diamond for Regard; Amethyst, Malachite, Jacinth, Turquoise, Jacinth and Emerald for Amitié; Lapis, Opal, Vermeil (a misnomer for a hessonite garnet), Emerald for Love. Sometimes the stones would be arranged in the form of a pansy flower called *pensée* in French, standing for 'think of the giver'. In the example illustrated, the flower head is cherished between the fingers of a pair of hands, giving an extra dimension to this already charming conceit. The fashion for these jewels reached a high point at the turn of the century but was partially eclipsed by the Revivalism which characterized the decorative arts from the 1840s onwards. Sometimes the message conveyed by gem-set rings is more directly understood, the bezels being set with conjoined heart-shaped rubies and diamonds, perhaps surmounted by a knot or a bow. Sometimes a single heart is seen crowned with diamonds or consumed with flames. These jewels are characterized by the finest of lapidary work in which the stones are specially cut to fit the composition.

The pansy flower ('*pensée*') stands for 'think of the giver'. The pansy in this gold ring, cherished between two finely modelled hands, is set with a Ruby, Emerald, Garnet, Amethyst, Ruby and Diamond, spelling REGARD. English, *c.* 1840. (*Mrs Stewart Munn.*)

The bezel of this gold ring is set with stones in the shape of twinned hearts: ruby for passion, diamond for constancy. The radiating background is decorated with emeralds, which may stand for hope. (*The Victoria and Albert Museum.*)

Below, a two-coloured gold pendant in the form of a basket of flowers, represented by Lapis-lazuli, Opal, Vermeil (a misnomer for hessonite garnet) and Emerald, spelling LOVE. Turquoise stands for forget-me-not and represents true love. English, *c.* 1840. (*Sandra Cronan, London.*)

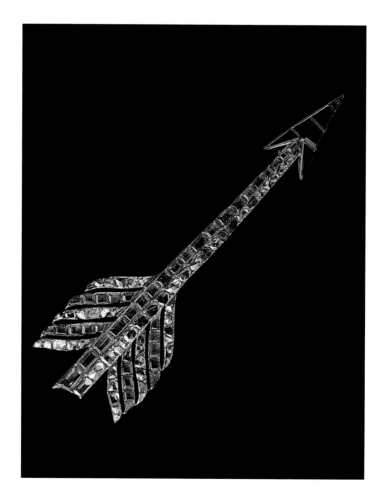

Cupid's arrow works well as a hair ornament, as in this silver jewel set with table cut emeralds and diamonds and flat cut garnets. French, *c.* 1700. (*By permission of the Trustees of the British Museum.*)

The wizened crone in this bitter *vanitas* by Goya, *Que tal?* (How do *you* feel?), dated 1796, is wearing a jeweled arrow similar to the one shown at left. (*Musée des Beaux-Arts, Lille.*)

There can be little doubt that of all the eighteenth-century love jewels those in the form of gem-set arrows are the most dramatic. An obvious reference to Cupid's dart, they were not popular before the turn of the seventeenth century. Typically they are set with diamonds or emeralds, but a larger number have survived in both white and coloured paste, and green chrysoberyl. Popular in Spain and particularly Portugal in the 1790s, one is worn in Goya's pitiless vanitas *Que tal?*, now in the Musée des Beaux-Arts, Lille.

Diamond-set arrows enjoyed a revival under France's Second Empire and were at their most chic in the form of *sûreté* pins made by Cartier to secure both hats and dresses during the first half of the twentieth century.

Opposite, this enamelled gold brooch seems to suggest a choice between love and the privileges of the bachelor life. A lady sitting at a window is being wooed by a soldier who carries a goblet and may be the worse for drink. The building is canopied with a trail of roses set with diamonds. The slightly ribald mood of the brooch is reminiscent of sixteenth-century Flemish jewels which were sometimes devoted to the difficulties of choice (see p. 25). French, *c.* 1800. (*John Joseph, London.*)

The Triumph of Love is symbolized in this oval gold locket by the heart-shaped stone surrounded by a laurel wreath tied with a bow. Decorated with enamel and set with diamonds, this neo-classical jewel is based on a late eighteenth-century design much favoured by the goldsmith James Morriset, who died in 1815. It was in fact made in the late nineteenth century and illustrates the wide-ranging eclecticism of the Victorian jeweler. English, *c.* 1880. (*Marilyn Meyers, New York.*)

Connubial life disdains a fragile toy
Which rust can tarnish, or a touch destroy,
Nor much admires, what courts the general gaze
The dazzling diamond's meretricious blaze
That hides, with glare, the anguish of the heart
By nature hard, tho' polished bright – by art.
  William Brennan, *The Wedding Ring*

Nineteenth-century jewelry design betrays a lack of self-confidence which is quite unwarranted. Artists were under the misconception that they had no direction of their own, and were obliged to return to the antique as the only safe source of inspiration.[15] This attitude was already apparent by the 1820s and, nurtured by the teachings of John Ruskin, was to dominate the aesthetics of the period. It is ironic that, with the benefit of hindsight, we see these revivalists as genuinely inspired in their own right and modern despite themselves.

Since it stood for Christian virtue and authority, the Gothic style was the first to be emulated by the Victorians, but it was quite incompatible with the classical sources which had been so important to the decoration of the eighteenth century. The architect of the Palace of Westminster, Augustus Welby Pugin (1812–52), gave his wife Jane a monumental Gothic parure of enamelled gold, set with garnets and pearls, when they were married in 1848. However, this was an exceptional gift; the jewelers who wanted their work to evoke sentiment

were forced to abandon not only prevailing tastes in decoration but also the brilliance of precious stones. Once again they resorted to coloured golds, enamel and the intimate language of flowers.[16] The forget-me-not is by far the best-known symbol of love in separation, but it also stands for 'true love', being only one of hundreds of meanings attributable, by ancient tradition, to the plant world. The Victorians enthusiastically revived this artificial system which is encapsulated in the following couplet by an un-named poet:

'The flowers in silence seem to breathe
Such thoughts as language cannot tell.'

Conveniently, the turquoise exactly parallels the colour of the forget-me-not; when the sky-blue stones are cut *en cabochon*, they represent the tiny petals of the flower and appear in abundance in every aspect of nineteenth-century jewelry design. Bridesmaids were traditionally given a dove of Venus pavé set with turquoise, sometimes carrying a heart in its beak, so that they would not easily forget the bride despite her new-found status. The theme was taken up by Queen Victoria when she married Prince Albert of Saxe-Coburg-Gotha in the Chapel Royal on 10 February 1840, but in this instance the bird is a Coburg Eagle in homage to the bridegroom's family.[17]

About forty years later Sir Edward Burne-Jones (1833–98) was to design his version of a bridesmaid's brooch, which was made up by Carlo Giuliano in the form of a turquoise and coral dove perched in an olive tree of green enamel emblematic of peaceful domesticity. The lilting quality of this jewel is an interesting contrast to Queen Victoria's somewhat aggressive eagle. Burne-Jones's version is contained within a heart-shaped red leather box, which emphasized its meaning. Turquoise is also seen in profusion on necklaces in the form of the *ouroboros*, or snake biting its tail; like the forget-me-not this ancient symbol stressed the metaphor of eternal love. All kinds of snake jewels were popular gifts in the nineteenth century, not least because they carried this covert yet fundamental message to the recipient. Sometimes they are decorated with enamel and carefully articulated in the manner of a Japanese *okimono*. More often, their aesthetic ancestry can be traced back to ancient Rome where, as bangles, they were worn on both the wrist and upper arm.

The salamander, which thrives as it burns, is a metaphor for passionate love. This large gold brooch is set with opals and demantoid garnets. English, *c.* 1890. (*Silver & Co., London.*)

A snake swallowing its tail is an ancient symbol of eternal love called the *Ouroboros*, a power that eternally consumes and renews itself. This elaborate example, an articulated gold necklace in the form of a snake which closes at the head and tail, is naturalistically enamelled, the eyes set with rubies. Geneva, *c.* 1840. (*Donohoe, London.*)

In the language of flowers, the daisy represents innocence. This gold brooch is naturalistically enamelled, the flower head *tremblant* and set with diamonds. The goldsmith, carefully observing nature, has even suggested a broken petal. French, *c.* 1880. (*Wartski, London.*)

The enamelled gold brooch (opposite) by Edward Tessier is in the form of a bouquet emblematic of married virtues. On the reverse is engraved 'WRC to AGMcK April 1871.' (*Private collection.*)

The turquoise is unusual in perfectly matching the petals of a flower. When another sort of bloom was wanted, the jeweler had to look elsewhere for a true representation of its colour, perhaps towards stained ivory or enamel. An enamel bouquet was made by Edward Tessier in about 1870 as a gift from groom to bride, each flower standing for an individual virtue. Needless to say, the rose, sacred to Venus, is placed centrally. Always a symbol of love, it carries no fewer that thirty-five related interpretations, depending on its variety and whether in bud or in bloom. The pansy, as we have already seen, stands for 'think of the giver' and is second only to the rose as an inspiration to goldsmiths. Mistletoe is 'a kiss' and was amusingly interpreted by Carlo Giuliano, the berry being carved from moonstone in the form of an *amorino*. Ivy is an emblem of fidelity and marriage, and is a rare but charming source of inspiration for brooches and sometimes even tiaras.[18] Daisies stand for innocence, and the enamelled brooch shown here is exceptional for its naturalism, which extends even to the broken petal on the top right of the flowerhead. Perhaps it is the lilac which carries the meaning most closely matched by the intensity of its colour, fragrance and transient beauty; it is the attribute of 'the first emotions of love' and was a particular favourite of the Empress Eugénie, wife of Napoleon III.[19] She purchased a diamond brooch in the form of a lilac spray from Maison Rouvenat at the Exposition Universelle in Paris in 1867. It cost 25,000 francs.

Just as flowers are the inspiration of love, so too is music. Mindful of this association, nineteenth-century jewelers made a wide range of miniature musical instruments decorated with coloured golds or set with precious stones. Among those reproduced here are lockets in the form of a mandolin and a hurdy-gurdy, but the lyre is more often found since it is the attribute of Orpheus who could charm wild beasts and even stones with his music. He, and by extension his lyre, are associated with unfailing devotion, since he followed his wife Eurydice even into the underworld. There he persuaded Hades to release her on condition that he never looked back to see if she was following. Unfortunately, he could not resist the temptation and lost her again.

The mistletoe was a symbol of fertility in the Celtic tradition; for the Victorians it signified a kiss and enjoyed a revival of popularity. This gold brooch is in the form of a mistletoe sprig, the leaves enamelled green; the berry, in the form of an *amorino* head, is carved from moonstone. By Carlo Giuliano, *c.* 1880. (*Private collection.*)

Music was part of the language of love for the Victorian jewelers. Below is a coloured gold brooch in the form of a lyre decorated with roses set with emeralds and an amethyst. (*S.J. Phillips, London.*)

Opposite, in Greek mythology, Orpheus transcended even death with his love for Eurydice. This gold pendant, emblematic of enduring love, is in the form of his head supported on the lyre with which he charmed the Lord of the Underworld. It was modelled by the archaeological jeweler Louis Wiese in Paris around 1890. (*S.J. Phillips, London.*)

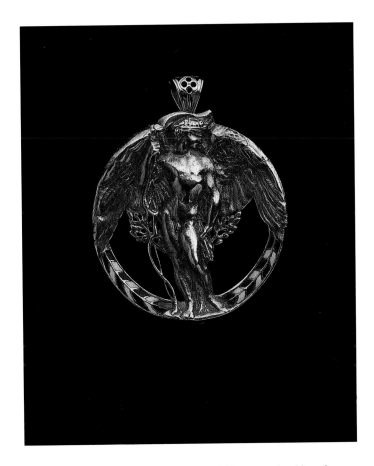

Above, Cupid blindfolded is the subject of this openwork gold pendant by Henry Wilson (1864–1934). The borders of the jewel are defined by the curve of Cupid's open wings and the crescent-shaped foreground which is decorated with green and white chevrons in the English medieval taste. This jewel is detachable from the back of a large rock crystal and gem-set tiara made by Wilson for Lady Llewellyn Smith in 1909. (*The Worshipful Company of Goldsmiths.*)

The proliferation of such musical instruments in nineteenth-century jewelry design may also be a reference to the opening words spoken by the Duke in Shakespeare's *Twelfth Night*: 'If music be the food of love, play on.' They are certainly an allusion to the harmony of love, a favourite conceit of the French neo-Renaissance goldsmith François-Désirée Froment-Meurice (1802–55), who represented the theme in a series of jewels made in the late 1840s. Typically they depict a muse within a Gothic niche bowing a viol while accompanied by *amorini* on the harp and triangle.[20]

In France in the mid-nineteenth century there was a revival of jewelry in the Renaissance tradition of clasped hands; they were worn as brooches, used to secure bracelets, and sometimes cast in solid gold as marriage seals. The matrices of the bride and groom were generally secured at the end of the wrists. Henri Vever records in his history of French nineteenth-century jewelry[21] that these charming ornaments were called 'bonne-foi' or 'mains touchées'. The more valuable examples were decorated with tiny gem-set rings and sometimes joined by the ancient symbol of snakes swallowing their own tails. The hands of the lovers are differentiated by jewelry and lace trimmings for ladies and starched cuff and buttons for men. Die-stamped versions were probably given as souvenirs at weddings.

Musical instruments are frequently used as symbols of harmony in amatory jewelry. Above is a coloured gold pendant in the form of a mandolin decorated with roses and forget-me-nots set with turquoise. Opposite is a small gold pendant in the shape of a hurdy-gurdy which opens to reveal compartments for souvenirs. The cover for the mechanism conceals an enamelled gold wheel decorated with the legend 'C'est toi qui m'inspire' (It's you who inspires me). English, *c.* 1840. (*Wartski, London.*)

Clasped hands representing lasting love appealed to Victorian sentimentality. Below is a pinchbeck marriage brooch in the form of the clasped hands of the bride and groom. (*Mrs Geoffrey Munn.*)

Right, a pair of bracelets in the form of lovers' hands joined by a snake biting its tail, the emblem for eternal love. The man's hand sports a ruby signet ring and a chased gold cuff, and the lady's an emerald ring on its forefinger and a bracelet set with a ruby, emerald and diamond. English, *c.* 1840. (*S.J. Phillips, London.*)

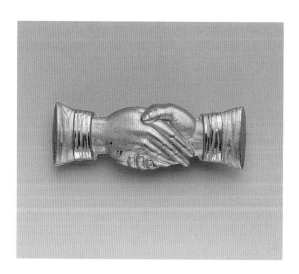

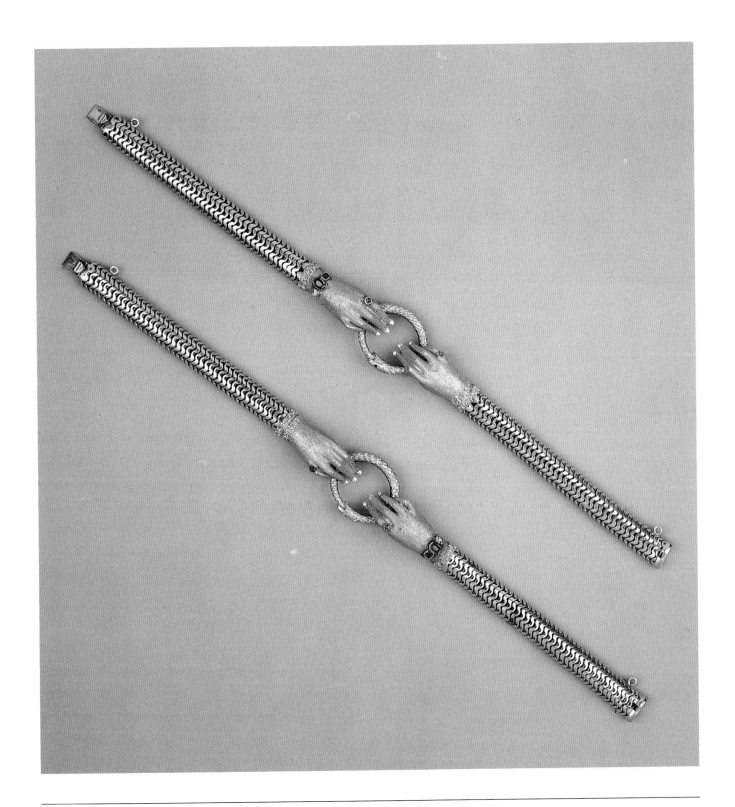

A portrait of Prince Albert by Queen Victoria in pencil and watercolour, and a portrait of Queen Victoria by Prince Albert in pencil, *c.* 1845. (*By Gracious Permission of Her Majesty the Queen.*)

Victorian sentimentality has been the object of much disparagement. That of the Queen herself was engendered by passionate love for her husband and commensurate grief when he died on 14 December 1861. The day after her wedding she wrote to her uncle King Leopold of the Belgians: 'Really I do not think it possible for anybody in the world to be happier or as happy as I am. He is an Angel . . . to look into those dear eyes, and that dear sunny face, is enough to make me adore him.'[22] The progress of their lives together was marked by gifts of jewelry on her birthday, his birthday, their anniversaries and every Christmas. Sometimes Albert designed the pieces himself. These presentations, however, were brought to an abrupt end after nine children and twenty-one years of marriage. Victoria wrote to her uncle again: 'My life as a happy one is ended! The world is gone from me!'[23] The grief-stricken Queen was soon to embark on a programme of tributes to her husband, which ranged in scale from the Albert Memorial in London to the inscribing of her large collection of jewelry with names and dates of presentation. Following the Queen's instructions, Princess Beatrice distributed a number of these jewels to friends and family after her death in 1901. Among them was a brooch in the form of a conventionalized heart in the Elizabethan taste surmounted by a crown of freshwater pearls, which had been given to the Queen by Prince Albert on 10 February 1843 to mark their third wedding anniversary. This was just nine months after the Spitalfields Ball which had been organized to revive the flagging London silk trade; Victoria and Albert were present as King Edward III and Queen Philippa. Albert had chosen the characters and designed the costumes for both himself and his wife. Victoria wore a crown in medieval taste, decorated with stylized leaves and fleur-de-lys, to which the wedding anniversary jewel is related in style. It is therefore tempting to suppose that Prince Albert played at least some part in the design and choice of stones. Certainly the Queen took pleasure in the gift, as she recorded in her journal.

Queen Victoria wrote of this jewel in her journal in 1843, 'My beloved Albert gave me a lovely brooch which is so original in design & which I am delighted with.' A present to mark their third wedding anniversary, it is engraved on the reverse 'From Albert Feby 10th 1843'. An openwork gold brooch in the Elizabethan taste, a stylized crowned heart decorated with Gothic foliage and surmounted by four freshwater pearls from Scotland, the jewel is set with amethysts, a garnet and two chrysoberyls. After the Queen's death in 1901 it passed to her daughter Princess Louise, Marchioness of Lorne. (*Private collection.*)

A pair of gold earrings by Giacinto Melillo in the form of *amorini* subduing the doves of Venus with silken cords. These and the jewel opposite, showing a cornucopia and an *amorino* playing the Pipes of Pan, also by Melillo, are based on Hellenistic prototypes and are decorated with granulation and filigree of exceptional quality. The revival of these ancient goldsmithing techniques has been credited principally to the Castellani family in Naples in whose workshop Melillo was trained. *c.* 1890. (*Private collection.*)

In 1863 William Burges (1827–81) pointed out that every goldsmiths' shop in London displayed 'Etruscan jewelry'[24]; we now realize that the widest possible interpretation was put on the word Etruscan, but his remark vividly demonstrates the fact that the London trade was preoccupied with what had come to be known as archaeological jewelry. As we have seen, the nineteenth-century designers had turned their attention to the Gothic, but they were also inspired by Greek, Roman and indeed Etruscan jewelry which was unearthed in unprecedented quantities throughout the century. Encouraged by the Castellani family of Rome and their mentor Michelangelo Caetani, Duke of Sermoneta (1804–82), the European jewelers were preoccupied not only with the design of classical jewelry but also the seemingly inimitable skills used in its manufacture. Amatory allusions are rarely found in archaeological jewelry, but when they do appear they derive from Greek mythology or Latin texts and are expressed in granulation, filigree, and micro-mosaic. Some typical examples are AEI (always or forever), UBI AMOR IBI ANIMA (Where love is, there is the soul), FIDES (faithfulness), SPES (hope), VITA (life).

Among the most charming nineteenth-century pastiches of Hellenistic jewelry is the series of *amorini* made by Castellani's pupil, Giacinto Melillo (1846–1915) in Naples. It was inspired by a type of earring common in antiquity, already discussed in the Introduction above.

Left, Psyche is the goddess of the soul and all higher emotions, including love. Her symbol is the butterfly, as can be seen in this gold brooch by Castellani in the archaeological taste. It is set with a micro-mosaic of a butterfly and the name Psyche appears below in Greek letters. On the reverse, the name of Eros can be seen in raised Greek letters. Rome, *c.* 1880. (*Private collection.*)

Two gold wishbone brooches emblematic of a wish and a hope. The one above was made by Carlo Giuliano, *c.* 1890. (*Private collection.*) The lower one is overlaid with a sprig of almond blossom, which stands for hope in the Victorian language of flowers. English, *c.* 1870. (*Wartski, London.*)

The ladder is an emblem of the aspirations of love. These two gold brooches of the mid-nineteenth century show complementary treatments of the symbol: on the one below two gold *amorini* are playing ball with tiny pearls. An enamel fly, an obscure symbol of humility, climbs the upright ladder. By Carlo Giuliano. (*Private collections.*)

Amorini are shown navigating boats and a raft in this silver and gold set of earrings and brooch. These charming jewels may refer to Shakespeare's sonnet 116: '[Love] is the star to every wandering bark.' By Marchesini of Florence, *c.* 1890. (*D.H. Edmonds, Brighton.*)

The fashion for neo-Renaissance jewelry was to run concurrently with the revival of earlier styles. In France, Froment-Meurice was well enough known for his work in the style to be called 'The Cellini of Paris'. In London, Castellani's pupil Carlo Giuliano (*c.* 1830–95) was responsible for the finest and most imaginative jewelry in the Renaissance taste. Among his most delightful pastiches is the brooch in the form of lovers navigating a sailboat, which is apparently another interpretation of Shakespeare's Sonnet No. 116. Giuliano also made numerous heart-shaped pendants and lockets, some of which are decorated with the heads of *amorini* or messages of love raised in letters of gold against an enamelled ground. Nonetheless, the training he received with Castellani meant that Giuliano's classical sources were among his favourites, even if executed in a medium unknown to the ancients.

Exactly like his mentor Pugin, the strange genius of William Burges found expression in every conceivable aspect of decoration. As we have already seen, goldsmiths' work and jewelry held a particular fascination for him, and a number of his brooches and pendants were of a sentimental nature. Sadly, none has been traced, but the watercolour designs which are preserved at the Victorian and Albert Museum give some idea of how they looked. Three of them are in the form of wreaths of oak and hawthorn, emblematic of strength and hope, and each is set with a heart-shaped cabochon garnet. These jewels are probably designed as wedding gifts and were made to the order of the architect J. R. Seddon and a certain Miss Tribe.

Burges's fellow architects C.F.A. Voysey (1857–1941) and Sir Edwin Lutyens (1869–1944) also involved themselves with jewelry design. The Rev. J. Tetley Rowe asked Voysey to design a marriage jewel; like Burne-Jones's, it was in the form of an enamelled gold tree in which the doves of Venus are perched. Lutyens used an elaborate painted wood-and-leather jewelry casket to win the hand of Lady Emily Lytton. Despite her social position and his uncertain prospects, its Pre-Raphaelite charm, expressed with briar roses, flaming hearts and *amorini*, persuaded Lady Emily of his sincerity and she asked her parents for permission to marry. The wedding took place on 4 August 1897.

Design for a brooch by William Burges: a pendant ruby heart surrounded by chased gold oak leaves, which represent strength. The brooch, which stands for the enduring qualities of true love, was to have been decorated with pearls. (*The Victoria and Albert Museum.*)

Opposite, an elaborate allegory of love by Carlo Giuliano. A gold brooch in the form of a sailboat, navigated by lovers with the doves of Venus perched on the prow. The sail is enamelled in royal blue against which are stars. Around the hull of the vessel is a band of oval cut precious stones, including emeralds, rubies, sapphires and rose diamonds. This dramatic jewel is probably based on the seventeenth-century conceit that love is the star by which the voyage through life is navigated. Signed C.G., *c.* 1875 (*The Cooper Hewitt, National Museum of Design, Smithsonian Institution, New York. Purchased in memory of Annie Schermerhorn Kane and Susan Dwight Bliss, 1969.*)

Above, heart-shaped pendant by Carlo and Arthur Giuliano decorated with opaque white and translucent red enamel against which the following legend is seen in gold letters, 'MON COEUR S'OUVRE A TA VOIX' (My heart opens at thy voice). This is a quotation from the opera *Samson and Delilah* by Saint-Saens which was performed in London in 1909; the jewel may have been made to celebrate the production. Provenance: Queen Alexandra. (*Private collection.*)

An openwork heart-shaped silver and gold pendant by Carlo and Arthur Giuliano, decorated with green and white enamels and set with cabochon sapphires. (*Private collection.*)

Courtly love was a seemingly inexhaustible source of inspiration to the Pre-Raphaelite artists, and was also the preoccupation of their personal lives. When Jane Burden married William Morris (1834–96) in 1859, she was given a wooden jewel casket bound in iron which Dante Gabriel Rossetti (1828–82) and Elizabeth Siddal had decorated with their own hands. Perhaps none of these artists was more romantically inclined than Burne-Jones and such tendencies were expressed by him in every conceivable medium, including designs for jewelry. A number of these survive at the Victoria and Albert Museum, the British Museum, and at Wightwick Manor in Wolverhampton. The majority are for brooches and pendants in the form of tied and flaming hearts or birds in trees, while some are in the Byzantine taste, decorated with pomegranates and *amorini*. Burne-Jones was fascinated not only by jewelry but also by the meaning of flowers and precious stones. He understood why the gold cross Ruskin commissioned him to design in 1883 for the May

Queen of Whitelands College in Chelsea had to be of hawthorn. It was an emblem of Ruskin's lost love for Rose La Touche, whose untimely death had driven him temporarily insane. Burne-Jones had also suffered when his great love Frances Graham abandoned him, albeit only to marry Sir John Horner. After deploring her choice of husband, Burne-Jones suggested that he himself should be awarded the hawthorn cross he was then designing for Ruskin, since he too needed consolation in his despair.

Burne-Jones wrote to Frances Horner on the subject of precious stones. He had invented a personal mythology and told her that

> *Ruby is passion, and I need it not. Emerald is hope and I need it . . . a diamond is strength and it sparkles and fidgets and is of this world. Amethyst . . . is devotion – I have it – and Topaz is jealousy, and is right nasty . . . Prase is a wicked little jewel, have none of him. I gave one to Margaret and it winked and blinked and looked so evil she put it away. And I got her a moonstone that she might never known love and stay with me. It did no good but was wonderful to look at – cold and desolate, and you sighed when you looked at it, as when you looked at the moon . . .*

Margaret was Burne-Jones's only daughter, of whom he was inordinately fond. Her favourite jewel was a 'poor cheap bit of ivory, stained so that it looked like a cherry.' Although Burne-Jones asked Giuliano to make the bridesmaid's brooches already mentioned (p. 63), he entrusted some of the less demanding work to a firm called Child and Child. Harold and Walter Child set a heart-shaped baroque pearl into a ring and green-stained ivory hearts in silver as cufflinks, both of which were for the artist's own use. It is clear that Burne-Jones's patronage had a profound effect on their commercial repertoire, since a considerable number of jewels made by the firm have a strongly Pre-Raphaelite accent. Invariably decorated with faience blue enamel, they are based on an ancient Egyptian amuletic device known as a winged globe which, when placed above the door of a house, protected the

Sir Edward Burne-Jones designed these cuff-links for his own use and they reflect his continued interest in the heart as a decorative device as well as a symbol of love. They were made by the jewelers Child and Child of green-stained ivory mounted in silver, and are marked with their monogram of two 'C's and a sunflower. (*Private collection.*)

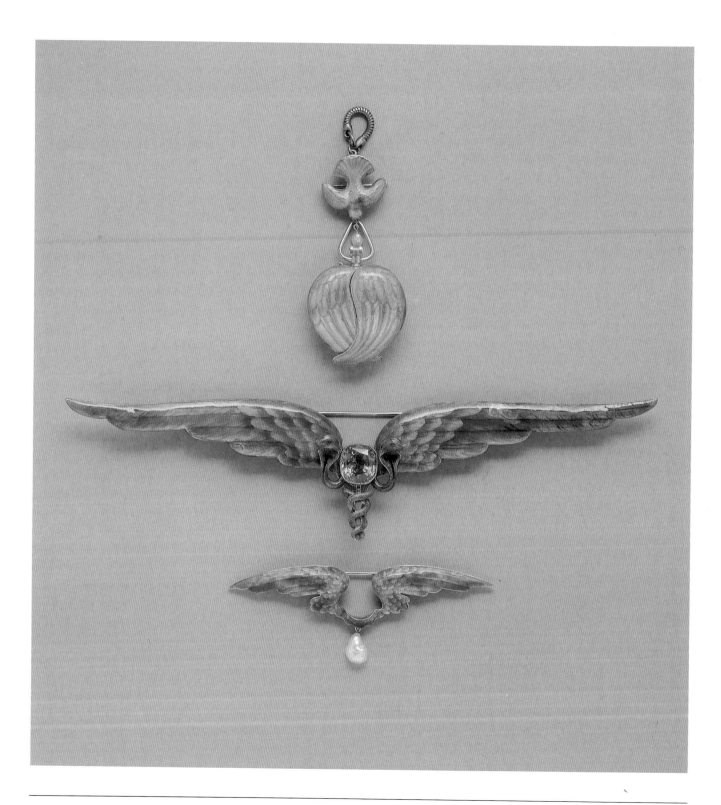

inhabitants from harm. By extension, their use in jewelry offered protection to the wearer. However, since the versions by Child and Child are usually centred on a heart or a brightly coloured gemstone, they are also emblematic of the wings of love. The watch reproduced here is part of a series and makes the association clear. The heart-shaped winged case opens to reveal the dial which stands for 'Tempus Fugit' (Time flies), while the legend 'Semper Amici' (Love remains) is clearly legible beneath the translucent blue enamel.

Vever has pointed out that the Pre-Raphaelites, most particularly William Morris and Burne-Jones, laid the foundations for what is now called the Art Nouveau movement.[26] Throughout Europe towards the end of the century, there was a reaction against revivalism; artists and designers were returning to nature for their inspiration. They had been given a lead by the large numbers of meticulously executed works of art being exported from Japan at the end of the Edo period. Siegfried Bing (1838–1905), who managed a shop specializing in modern design in Paris, had written in the introductory article to the first issue of *La Japon Artistique*, dated May 1888: 'This art is permanently bound together with ours. It is like a drop of blood that has mingled with our blood, and now no power on earth is able to separate it again.' Certainly the European goldsmith was never to be the same once he had been influenced by Japanese enamels, patinated metals, and the unselfconscious use of organic materials including ivory, tortoiseshell and horn.

A butterfly carrying away a *putto*: probably an allusion to Psyche (symbolized by the butterfly) and Cupid, except that it is usually Cupid who is in pursuit of the goddess of the soul. The brooch is made of gold, the butterfly of hardstone with ruby and diamond-set wings. Possibly Viennese, *c.* 1890. (*Camille Dietz Bergeron, Ltd., New York.*)

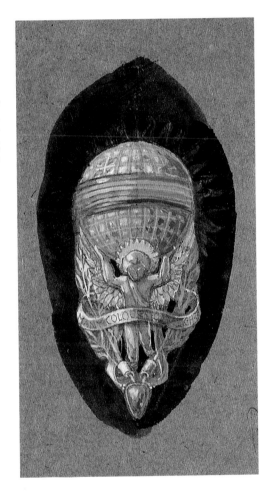

A design by Edward Spencer for the Artificers' Guild featuring an *amorino* in the guise of Atlas. The globe he holds up is circled by a rainbow and the whole is supported on a triumphal laurel tied with a ribbon which reads: 'Many colours, one light.' (*The Worshipful Company of Goldsmiths.*)

A neo-classical onyx cameo of Psyche and Cupid by Tommaso Saulini (1793–1864) after a basrelief by John Gibson now in the Royal Academy of Arts, London. The gem was carved in Rome between 1844 and 1854 and mounted as a brooch in gold with the addition of brilliant cut diamonds. Gibson wrote of his original sculpture to the Duke of Northumberland: 'It is the soul pursued by desire.'
(*Wartski, London.*)

A cameo of *putti* playing a game of Blind Man's Buff, an allegory of the arbitrary nature of love. The cameo is set into an oval openwork gold brooch by Carlo Giuliano, decorated with black and white *champlevé* enamel and set with eight brilliant diamonds. London, *c.* 1880. (*Private collection.*)

Cupid is subduing the lions in an agate cameo by Niccolo Morelli. This charming jewel, set in the lid of an engraved gold box, is an allegory of the triumph of love over strength. *c.* 1820.
(*Wartski, London.*)

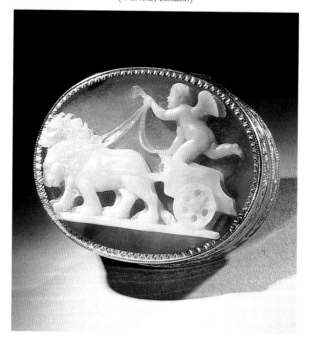

Opposite, a gold pendant and chain, showing lovers embracing within a bower of ivy, the berries set with diamonds. The faces of the lovers are carved from ivory. Ivy, which is green in winter, is a symbol of the enduring qualities of love. This jewel is typical of the elaborate yet delicate work of René Lalique, the master of Art Nouveau jewelry. Paris, *c.* 1900. (*The Lalique Museum, Japan. Photograph: The Worshipful Company of Goldsmiths.*)

The return to nature resulted in a rejection of the antique. A primitive and sensual quality was more often found in jewelry design, and the most imaginative work was by René Lalique (1860–1945). Metaphors for love were rejected in favour of an often morbid eroticism, in which women were associated with the insect world, sleep and death, metamorphosis, and even sapphism. A series of pendant jewels in glass and enamel were made by Lalique called 'The Kiss'. Even though they paralleled the work of the painter Edvard Munch and the sculptor Auguste Rodin, they were considered daring and were quite without precedent in the history of jewelry design.

It was only in Russia that the allegory of love still preocuppied the goldsmith and jeweler. There the restless imagination of Carl Fabergé (1846–1920) was to give new style and vigour to the final interpretation of an ancient theme. What had seemed an inexhaustible source of inspiration was to have less and less relevance in a machine age, marked by revolution and teetering on the edge of war.

A rare Art Nouveau treatment of the doves of Venus. This gold brooch is set with diamonds, rubies and a pearl; the doves are naturalistically represented in opalescent and *plique-à-jour* enamel. Probably Austrian, *c.* 1900. (*Christie's Amsterdam.*)

The Triumph of Love is summed up by this platinum brooch in the form of a ruby and diamond heart pierced with three similarly decorated arrows. The heart is circled with laurels. French, *c.* 1900.
(*Young and Stephen Ltd., London.*)

Opposite, a neo-classical diamond-set head ornament by Carl Fabergé mounted in gold and set in silver in the form of a wreath of myrtle. Myrtle leaves and berries were sacred to Aphrodite and Fabergé's use of them in the design of this elegant jewel suggests that it may have been made for a bride of the Grosvenor family. Signed KO, *c.* 1900.
(*Their Graces the Duke and Duchess of Westminster.*)

This gold brooch by Carl Fabergé is emblematic of love: a gold heart set with sapphires and overlapped by twinned mistletoe sprigs set with diamonds. St Petersburg, *c.* 1900.
(*Private collection.*)

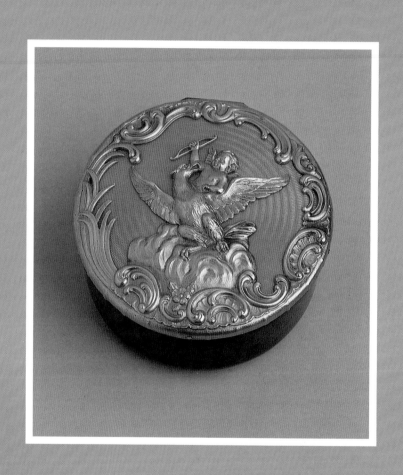

Cupid is subduing a phoenix on
the gold and pink guilloché
enamelled lid of this circular
nephrite snuff box by Fabergé.
The symbolism is love revived,
since the mythical phoenix has
traditionally been associated with
hope and renewal. St Petersburg,
c. 1903. Stamped with the marks
of both Henrik Wigstrom and
Michael Perchin.
*(Miss Joan Rivers and Miss Melissa
Warburg Rosenberg, New York.)*

'Remember' is the message in
diamond-set Cyrillic initials
(POMNI) on this square
openwork gold brooch with a
conventionalized fleur-de-lys at
each corner. By Carl Fabergé,
workmaster Oskar Pihl.
Moscow, *c.* 1880.
(Mrs A. Kenneth Snowman.)

And when, throughout all the wild orgasms of love
slowly a gem forms, in the ancient, once-more molten rocks
of two human hearts, two ancient rocks, a man's heart and a woman's
that is the crystal of peace, the slow hard jewel of trust,
the sapphire of fidelity.
The gem of mutual peace emerging from the wild chaos of love.
D.H. Lawrence, *Fidelity*

The Ritz Hotel in London, which opened in 1905, was lavishly decorated in the Louis XV taste by Mewès and Davies. Even today visitors will be struck by its lavish decorations in rose Pompadour and pure gold, and it seems that every available surface is dedicated to Aphrodisian themes. The Honourable Mrs Ronald Greville, a close friend of the Royal Family, chose the same architects to refurnish the interior of her home, Polesden Lacey, in Surrey.

Mrs Greville was an enthusiast of Fabergé's work and must have seen in it a reflection of her taste in interior design. The Russian goldsmith was an eclectic genius and a good proportion of his work is based on the revival of pre-Revolutionary French decoration. Garlands of roses in four-coloured gold are used to embellish all manner of objects, and the ubiquitous lamp of love and Cupid's quiver are used to surmount photograph frames of enamelled gold, Siberian jade or perhaps grey Kalgan jasper. Such objects were considered ideally pitched as gifts to King Edward VII and Queen Alexandra; as a result the Royal Collection at Sandringham is uniquely comprehensive. Mrs Greville gave a number of them and received several in return, which are preserved to this day by the National Trust at Polesden Lacey. She had been

Below, this diamond set gold brooch was a gift from Edward VII to his friend the Hon. Mrs George Keppel. It is in the form of a snake guarding a large red tourmaline; the eyes are set with rubies. The snake biting its tail is a traditional symbol of eternal love. English, *c.* 1890. (*Private collection.*)

introduced to the King by one of his closest friends, the Honourable Mrs George Keppel. Alice Keppel was amiable, witty and generous, and she was inspired in her choice of gifts. It was she who suggested to Fabergé that the Royal pets and farmyard animals should be modelled by the Russian lapidaries in hardstone, and that Balmoral and Sandringham should be painted in enamel on gold and framed in Siberian jade. The King showed his affection for her with gifts of goldsmiths' work and jewelry. Among them was a large red tourmaline guarded by a diamond-set snake biting its tail, which was a mark of his eternal regard. It is a tribute to Mrs Keppel's charm and Queen Alexandra's magnanimity that she was invited to the King's bedside just before he died in 1910.

The arrow in jewelry, emblematic of Cupid's armoury, continued into the twentieth century. Here it appears in an unusually large gold and silver brooch entirely set with diamonds. It is accompanied by three diamond set sureté pins of the same form, one of which is decorated with calibre cut emeralds. Probably French, *c.* 1925. (*Johnson Walker & Tolhurst & Katherine Purcell.*)

The greatest of Fabergé's competitors both in London and in St Petersburg was the firm of Cartier. Before the Russian Revolution, they supplied the Imperial Court with jewelry as well as *objets d'art*, and were the particular favourite of the Grand Duchess Vladimir, whose passion for precious metalwork was legendary. Just as Fabergé had done, Cartier turned to eighteenth-century France for inspiration; this resulted in a decorative scheme which has come to be known as the garland style because of the trails of diamond-set flowers which characterize it. From time to time the lovers' knot is expressed in openwork diamond bows set in platinum and made to decorate the corsage; sometimes Cupid's dart gleams from the brim of a hat decorated with the plumes of osprey or bird of paradise. It is unlikely that even the owners of these jewels

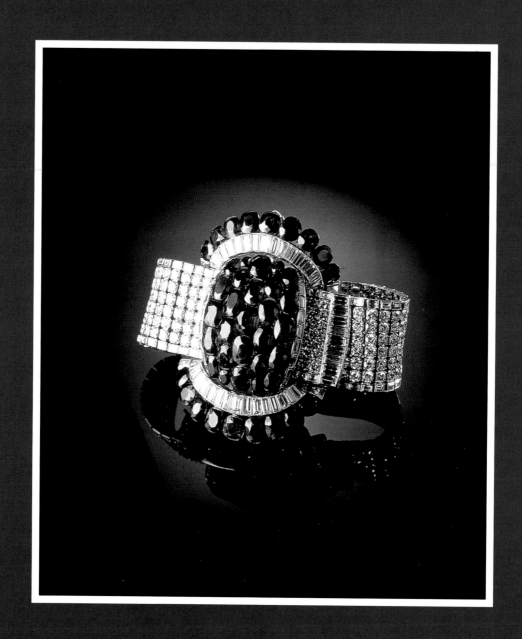

Opposite, given by the Duke of Windsor to Mrs Simpson, this bracelet is known as the marriage contract bracelet. He bought the jewel in May 1937 and the document of marriage was drawn up on the 18th of that month in Monts (Indre-et-Loire), France. The sapphire and diamond *jarretière* bracelet was designed by René-Sim Lacaze and made by the Paris house of Van Cleef and Arpel. (*Sotheby's.*)

A Cartier brooch in the form of a Musubikiri knot which, by Japanese tradition, cannot easily be untied. It symbolizes an event in life which by its nature should not be repeated. Love and marriage are typical examples. The openwork platinum and gold jewel is set with rubies and diamonds. Paris, 1907. (*The Cartier Museum, Geneva.*)

were aware of their meaning, which had been eclipsed yet again by the material from which they were made. There are, however, some rare exceptions. In 1910, Cartier mounted a large blue heart-shaped diamond of 30.82 carats as a corsage ornament.[27] The sizeable white brilliants that surround it were in settings designed as lilies-of-the-valley, which are emblematic of Love Revived. The piece was created for Mrs Unsue of Argentina.

In 1907 a ruby and diamond brooch was designed by Cartier in the form of a Japanese knot, which was thought to bring good luck at weddings. Its geometric lines anticipate the Art Deco movement of the early 1920s and early '30s.

Mrs Wallis Simpson, later Duchess of Windsor, was an enthusiast of both modern jewelry and the Art Deco style. Throughout their lives together, the Duke showered her with presents from Cartier, Van Cleef and Arpels, Belperron and Harry Winston. They were an expression of the love which endured in spite of extraordinary difficulties. A good proportion of them were engraved with messages of endearment in facsimile of the Duke's handwriting and these were invariably dated too. Such attention to detail was something which may have come down to him from his great-grandmother Queen Victoria, but it may also have been an expression of the insecurity which had marked his entire life. After the death of

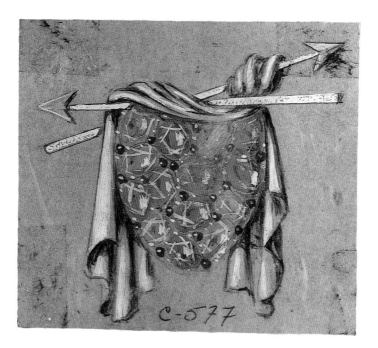

In the mid-twentieth century, Fulco di Verdura designed a number of love tokens in the shape of a heart. The design (left) for a brooch in the form of a trophy of love shows a pink tourmaline and ruby heart draped with a gold banner and surmounted by a pair of diamond-set arrows with gold heads. The large heart-shaped gold box (right) is set with pink tourmalines and aquamarines. (*Verdura, New York.*)

the Windsors, their jewelry collection was sold at auction in 1987 on behalf of the Pasteur Institute in Paris. The very high prices achieved for even the most modest of souvenirs reflected the public's interest in a King who had abandoned his duty and given up his throne for love.

Some of the Duke and Duchess's more imaginative commissions were given to the eccentric Fulco Santostefano della Cerda, Duke of Verdura and Marquess of Murata la Cerda – who was known professionally simply as 'Verdura'. Having spent his inheritance on a single fancy dress party soon after his father's death, Verdura left his native Sicily for Paris, where he became a dress designer for Chanel. It was there that he embarked on a range of personal ornaments which were an unconventional combination of large precious and semi-precious gemstones and enamel arranged in startling designs. In 1937 he transferred the business to New York and eventually opened premises on Fifth Avenue which attracted the attention of that arbiter of fashion, Diana Vreeland, whose recommendation assured his success.

Probably as a result of his unusual background, Verdura's work derives from a bewildering range of sources

and is exotic as well as romantic. Hearts, both pierced and
chained, and sometimes winged, are favourite themes; lovers
embrace and Cupid is seen riding a dolphin, sacred to his
mother Venus. These are neo-Renaissance jewels, the last of a
tradition of love jewelry broken only by the commercial
jewelers of today. The reasons for this hiatus are not obvious;
designers and goldsmiths seem ashamed to articulate the
feelings of lovers lest they be accused of sentimentality and bad
taste. With the gradual levelling of society, perhaps the lovers
themselves feel that modern jewelry is beyond their reach and
diminished standards make the majority of what is available
unworthy.

However, as we approach the turn of another century in
an increasingly precarious world, there is a revival of interest
in craftsmanship and decoration, and a renewed respect for the
affairs of the heart. Modern goldsmiths and jewelers will
undoubtedly realize that the austerity of the twentieth century
is the exception to an ancient rule and will wish to return to the
subject which has consistently inspired their delightful trade
for the last four hundred years.

The message on the hexagonal
gold pendant set with kite-
shaped sapphires and decorated
with enamel is 'Je vous couvre
de 1000 baisers' (I cover you
with 1000 kisses). French,
c. 1920. (*Private collection.*)

NOTES

1. F.H. Marshall *Catalogue of the Jewellery Greek, Etruscan, and Roman in the Department of Antiquities, British Museum*, London 1911, pp. 199–204.
2. *Ibid.*, no. 1984.
3. Yvonne Hackenbroch *Renaissance Jewellery*, London 1979, p. 3.
4. Hugh Ross Williamson *Lorenzo the Magnificent*, London 1974, pp. 93–112.
5. Hugh Tait *Catalogue of the Waddesdon Bequest in the British Museum*, vol. I: The Jewels, London 1986, pp. 79–84.
6. Yvonne Hackenbroch and Maria Sprameli *I Gioielli dell'Elettrice Palatina al Museo degli Argenti*, Florence 1988, pp. 70–72.
7. Roy Strong and Julia Trevelyan Oman *Elizabeth R*, London 1971, p. 7.
8. Hackenbroch *op. cit.*, p. 293.
9. Diana Scarisbrick, 'Anne of Denmark's Jewellery Inventory', *Archaeologia*, vol. CIX, London 1991.
10. *Treasures and Trinkets. Jewellery in London from Pre-Roman Times to the 1930's*, compiled by Tessa Murdoch, Museum of London, London, 1991, p. 44.
11. *Princely Magnificence. Court Jewels of the Renaissance 1500–1630*, Victoria and Albert Museum, London 1980, no. 75b.
12. Joan Evans *A History of Jewellery 1100–1870*, London 1953, p. 149.
13. Tait *op. cit.*
14. A. Kenneth Snowman *Eighteenth Century Gold Boxes of Europe*, Woodbridge (U.K.) 1990, p. 187.
15. Alessandro Castellani *Antique Jewellery and Its Revival*, London 1862.
16. Anna C. Burke *Illustrated Language of Flowers*, London 1856; Kate Greenaway *Language of Flowers*, London 1884.
17. Diana Scarisbrick *Ancestral Jewels*, London 1987, p. 126.
18. Charlotte Gere and Geoffrey C. Munn *Artists' Jewellery – Pre-Raphaelite to Arts and Crafts*, Woodbridge 1984, pp. 54–57.
19. Henri Vever *La Bijouterie française au 19ème siècle*, Paris 1908, vol. II, p. 289.
20. Hugh Tait (ed.) *The Art of the Jeweller. A Catalogue of the Hull-Grundy Gift to the British Museum*, London 1984, no. 1019.
21. Vever *op. cit.*
22. Arthur Benson and Viscount Esher (eds.) *The Letters of Queen Victoria*, 3 vols, London 1908, vol. I, p. 217.
23. *Ibid.*, vol. III, p. 473.
24. William Burges, 'Antique Jewellery and Its Revival', *The Gentleman's Magazine*, XIV, London 1863, p. 403.
25. Frances Horner *Time Remembered*, London 1933, pp. 121–23.
26. Vever *op. cit.*, vol. III, p. 752.
27. Hans Nadelhoffer *Cartier, Jewelers Extraordinary*, London 1984, p. 289.

BIBLIOGRAPHY

The most comprehensive bibliography of the history of jewelry is to be found in *The Art of the Jeweller – A Catalogue of the Hull-Grundy Gift to the British Museum*, by Charlotte Gere, Judy Rudoe, Hugh Tait and Timothy Wilson (British Museum Publications, London 1984). For the purposes of this study only a handful of publications need to be added to it, and they are as follows:

Vivienne Becker *Art Nouveau Jewellery*, London/New York 1985
Shirley Bury *An Introduction to Sentimental Jewellery*, London 1985
—— *Jewellery 1789–1910 – The International Era*, Woodbridge 1991
Beatriz Chadour and Rudiger Joppien *Schmuck I, Schmuck II*, Cologne 1985
Grosvenor House Antiques Fair (Handbook), London 1983: *Queen of the Dressing Table – Madame de Pompadour's Jewellery*
Lisette Hansmann and Lenz Kriss Rettenbeck *Amulet und Talisman*, Munich 1977
Tessa Murdoch *Treasures and Trinkets. Jewellery in London from Pre-Roman Times to the 1930's*, London 1991
Diana Scarisbrick *Ancestral Jewels*, London 1989
—— 'Joining Hands in a Ring', *Country Life*, 24 July 1986
—— 'Rewards of Discretion – The Jewels of Mrs. Keppel', *Country Life*, 11 May 1987
—— 'Message of Fidelity', *Country Life*, 7 April 1988
—— 'Public and Private Jewels', *Country Life*, 13 October 1988
Tait, Hugh *Catalogue of the Waddesdon Bequest in the British Museum*, vol. I, The Jewels, London 1986

Special mention should also be made of Mario Praz, *Studies in Seventeenth Century Imagery* (2nd ed.), Rome 1964, which provides an invaluable analysis of the art of the emblematist and a list of emblem books.

'Gems and Jewellery in Victorian Fiction' by Kurt Tetzeli von Rosador in *Real – The yearbook of Research in English and American Literature*, vol. 2, 1984, is an excellent study of the emblematic function of jewellery in 19th-century England.

ACKNOWLEDGMENTS

I am grateful to Her Majesty The Queen for gracious permission both to quote from Queen Victoria's journal and to reproduce various works of art and jewellery from the Royal Collection. Shirley Bury has been most generous with her time and knowledge, particularly with reference to the jewel which the Prince Consort gave Queen Victoria on their third wedding anniversary. Charlotte and John Gere have offered help and encouragement throughout this project. So too have Yvonne Hackenbroch, Jack Ogden, John Goodall, and Judy and Gyora Novak. Lady de Bellaigue and Frances Dimond of the Royal Archives at Windsor have been patient beyond the call of duty. Ernesto de Carolis organized the photography of the fresco at the Casa dei Vettii at Pompeii. Katherine Purcell has placed her extraordinary linguistic skills at my disposal and has taken up the challenge of transforming a scarcely legible manuscript into a neatly presented text.

It was Stanley Baron of Thames and Hudson who commissioned me to write this small book and he has also been a sensitive and tactful editor. My colleagues at Wartski, June Trager and Peter Cant have helped in ways too varied to describe.

Kenneth Snowman has given me the benefit of his intimate knowledge of precious metalwork on an almost daily basis. Furthermore, he has allowed me to reproduce plates from his book *Eighteenth Century Gold Boxes of Europe*. I am deeply indebted to those owners who have allowed me to reproduce objects from their collections but have preferred to remain anonymous.

Lastly, my thanks to Caroline, my wife, the mother of Alexander and Edward, to whom this book is dedicated.

INDEX